THE AMERICAN HEROIN EMPIRE

Power, Profits, and Politics

Also by Richard Kunnes, M.D.

YOUR MONEY OR YOUR LIFE:
An Indictment of the Medical Market Place

THE
AMERICAN
HEROIN
EMPIRE

POWER, PROFITS, AND POLITICS

By RICHARD KUNNES, M.D.

DODD, MEAD & COMPANY
NEW YORK

ISBN: 0–396–06697–6
Library of Congress Catalog Card Number: 72–3930

Printed in the United States of America
by The Cornwall Press, Inc., Cornwall, N. Y.

All through the sixties the dope flew free
Thru Tan Son Nhut Saigon to Marshall Ky
Air America following through
Transporting comfiture for President Thieu.
All these dealers were decades and today
The Indochinese mob of the CIA.

—Excerpt from "CIA Dope Calypso"
by Allen Ginsberg

Contents

1 Heroin and Health: An Epidemic of Junk

The American heroin empire is literally just that, an empire based on heroin. The empire involves American governmental officials, important foreign political figures in numerous countries, as well as the Mafia and organized crime. The empire also includes numerous American industries and institutions. The empire is a worldwide operation, complete with colonies and client states, with expeditionary forces and foreign markets.

Ultimately, the empire and its markets are controlled by merchants of death. Heroin has become *the* major killer of young people between the ages of eighteen and thirty-five, outpacing death from accidents, suicides, or cancer. Three to four addicts die every day in New York City alone.

And yet the drug itself, heroin, is relatively harmless.

As Dr. Joel Fort, former consultant on drug abuse to the World Health Organization says: "Heroin is a hard drug only in the sense that the addiction is very strong. Chronic excessive use of heroin produces *no physical damage at all.*"

1

Cigarettes and alcohol, on the other hand, cause respectively forty thousand deaths per year from lung cancer and fifty thousand deaths per year from alcoholic cirrhosis. A film sponsored by the National Institute of Mental Health on alcoholism said that "the host who insists on keeping guests' glasses filled at all times is not a good host but a pusher."

Heroin, in its pure and unadulterated state, does not produce organic, bodily damage. Addicts on quality heroin could function quite well, safely and effectively, other than the hour or so they would be "nodding," (i.e., dozing, following injection of the heroin).

However, the extreme profitability of the drug, because of the illegality and criminality associated with it, insures that heroin merchants will routinely dilute and adulterate the heroin, so that by the time it reaches the addict consumer, it is of an uneven quality and quantity. The most common dilutant is sugar; adulterants range from amphetamines to strychnine to rat poison. In effect, when the addict "shoots up," he or she is never sure how much of what gets into his/her veins, and thus deaths routinely occur.

An additional cause of addict fatalities is from infection, secondarily to unsterilized needles. The illegality of heroin insures that addicts will have unsterile needles.

According to Dr. Louis Weinstein, one of the country's leading infectious disease experts, "In some municipal hospitals one out of every ten patients is said to be an addict with a serious infection. They often spend weeks, even months, at base costs of $100 a day in Bellevue, Harlem, and similar municipal hospitals throughout the country. Tens of millions of dollars are spent each year for the care of such patients." Of course, as the addicts pass the needles and syringes around, they spread the bug.

Aside from the danger of infection, heroin purchased on the street is extremely expensive, regardless of its adulterated state. Such expenses leave the addict constantly short of money and thus short of food. Therefore, it is not surprising that malnutrition is a major source of heroin addict morbidity.

The addict, always poor and thus always malnourished, is highly susceptible to infections, not only from protein deficiencies but from unsterile, contaminated needles. The addict will do anything for money, regardless of whether it's harmful to himself/herself or to others. For example, because of an increasing utilization of expensive medical technology such as open-heart surgery, the demand for blood has doubled in the last decade. This increased demand for blood has strained traditional methods of collection and forced many hospitals to rely on commercial sources, which in turn will use, as their prime sources of blood, addicts looking for twenty-five dollars for a pint of their blood. Not only does this weaken the addict further, but, when the blood is transfused into the patient-recipient, it also transfuses into the recipient the addict's hepatitis, syphilis, and/or malaria for which there is no really adequate screening. Since 70 to 80 percent of all blood transfused in the United States now comes from such commercial sources, it is not surprising that in 1970 alone thirty-thousand Americans contracted hepatitis from contaminated transfusions, of whom over fifteen hundred died.

Another example of the addict not being the only victim of his/her addiction is seen in the case of addicted pregnant women. Because of the heroin in the mother's bloodstream passing into the baby's, the baby is born an addict and if not treated quickly will suffer a fatal heroin withdrawal, in effect going "cold turkey" at birth. Adequate prenatal care, however, removes the problem. Of course such care is virtually nonexistent for poor women, and virtually all women addicts are poor. In Harlem Hospital addicts give birth to one in every twenty-nine babies, i.e., one in twenty-nine babies at that hospital is born addicted.

In spite of the assertions from many politicians and physicians that keeping heroin illegal keeps its accessibility and thus the number of addicts limited, just the opposite seems to be the case. It is precisely the illegality of heroin that insures not only its profitability, but ultimately its accessibility.

Heroin, as a product, yields a pleasurable effect for the consumer, and creates the desire, or better still for the purveyor, the need for repeated use. The ideal commercial nature of heroin lies in the fact that each dosage incorporates a built-in obsolescence. No sales talk is necessary. The consumer will crawl through a sewer and beg to buy.

When the product is scarce it is therefore susceptible to a higher markup in price. As any college economics major knows, any profit-intensive market has an impetus to expand, in this case to create new addicts as rapidly and as frequently as possible. On the other hand, a nonprofit market would have no impetus for expansion. The heroin market will remain profitable as long as it remains illegal, and as long as it remains profitable, it will remain accessible and expanding.

The best and most efficient method for an addict to insure continuing financial support for his habit is for him to become a pusher himself, to start friends and associates on heroin, and to create a new heroin minimarket controlled by himself.

As the U.S. Attorney for the Southern District of New

York, Whitney N. Seymour, Jr., points out: "The evidence is: most addict recruits are introduced to heroin by their peers."

Dr. Judianne Densen-Gerber, director of Odyssey House, a rehabilitation center for addicts, says "addiction is a communicable disease."

Myles Ambrose of the Justice Department's Office of Drug Abuse says, "an addict tries to get another person to become an addict. It is the most contagious disease there is." Of course this can and does go on in ever-widening cycles. Not surprisingly, the number of addicts has increased year after year for the last twenty years without exception.

To get a picture of how the heroin market might expand and expand and how the number of addicts might increase year after year, let's examine an imprecise, yet interesting, possible mathematical model of the heroin market. If we start with, say, 1950, as year number one, with only one heroin addict, what happens if that addict becomes a small-time pusher and creates one new addict a year every year? And what happens if that new addict himself becomes a minipusher and creates one new addict a year every year and so on until 1970?

YEAR	NUMBER OF ADDICT-PUSHERS
1950	1
1951	2
1952	4
1953	8
1954	16
1955	32
1956	64
1957	128
1958	256
1959	512
1960	1000 (rounded off)
1961	2000

```
1962..............4000
1963..............8000
1964..............16,000
1965..............32,000
1966..............64,000
1967..............128,000
1968..............256,000
1969..............500,000 (rounded off)
1970..............1,000,000
```

At the very least this model shows how little it would take to create a heroin epidemic. Giving some credence to this model, Dr. Jerome Jaffe, director of the White House's Drug-Abuse Program, cited the example of how in one small town in 1965 there was one heroin user who "infected six other persons in 1966 and that the number expanded to 13 in 1967."

Given a potential market of fifty million poor and alienated people looking for a way out of their misery, and small-time pushers looking for new customers because illegalization of heroin forces them to, in order to support their own habit, it wouldn't take much to make the above figures a reality.

According to the Justice Department's Office of Drug Abuse: "If our *present rate* of growth of heroin addiction in the United States continues through the '70's and '80's we will have a nation with many millions of heroin addicts." A problem of this magnitude has obvious inferences for law-enforcement officials. As U.S. Attorney Whitney N. Seymour, Jr., observes: "As long as there is a *steadily growing*, [emphasis added] body of addicts with billions of dollars to steal and to spend for heroin on the illegal market, effective enforcement will be an almost impossible task."

From the market point of view, heroin, in spite of its scarcity, must nevertheless be available and the supply reasonably reliable for multilevel, multinational business transactions to occur. The product should not be subject to deterioration and should have a high value per unit of weight. Heroin meets these criteria extremely well, and thus is an ideal contraband product.

Scarcity is assured by official suppression of heroin, though the suppression is limited and discretional. The supply of heroin, on the other hand, is reliable, since fluctuations owing to opium crop failure or confiscation are easily overcome, either by reserves on hand, or by varying the degree of dilution and adulteration of the final product. As David Feingold points out in *Laos: War and Revolution*, ". . . opium derivatives [i.e., heroin] are stable and may be easily stored for long periods, without fear of deterioration . . ." and with the expectation that the price of heroin will continue to be inflated. Actually, the older opium becomes, the more it is worth.

2 Building the Heroin Empire

Where does heroin come from and how does it get to our streets? And why have all the attempts made at controlling heroin distribution failed, and why will they continue to fail? First of all, and contrary to popular myth, most opium, from which heroin is derived, is not grown in the Middle East, but in Southeast Asia.

According to the United Nations Commission on Drugs and Narcotics, since at least 1966 "80 percent of the world's illicit opium comes from Southeast Asia."

The opium plant, the poppy, is a sturdy plant and can be grown in many different climates. Then why is there such a continuing and expanding concentration of opium agriculture in the Far East? The answer to this is directly related to the trafficking and distribution routes of heroin. The countries directly involved are Laos, Thailand, Burma, Cambodia, and Vietnam. What do all these countries have in common, besides a flourishing opium crop? What they have in common are nationalistic and anti-American insurgencies. The insurgents and the insurgencies they wage, in one form or another, aid and abet the Viet Cong in the Vietnamese rebellion. These insurgents in the countries which surround Vietnam, i.e., Laos, Thai-

8

land, Burma, and Cambodia, are the local counterparts of the Viet Cong and the National Liberation Front. The United States, fearing two, three, many Vietnams, wishes to suppress these rebellions before they require a further increase in the investment of American military resources. To limit the expenditure of American lives, in the United States attempt to control these rebellions, Asian mercenaries are being hired and supported primarily by the U.S. Central Intelligence Agency (CIA), and to a lesser degree by the U.S. Agency for International Development (AID). Unfortunately, many of the mercenaries hired, such as the Meo tribes in Laos, have been and are a major international source of the world's opium. Thus, the United States, in its public position on heroin, is devoted to eliminating the drug, but in its practice is actively and knowingly supporting heroin production through its support of the Meo tribes and other United States-supported, opium-producing mercenaries.

As a case in point, the Meo poppy growers of Laos were selected by the CIA as its counterinsurgency bulwark against the Communist-oriented Pathet Lao guerrillas. While other areas of Laos often constituted "free fire zones," the Meo's mountain bastion safely received refugees from throughout Laos. Many of the refugees were, and are being, kept busy growing poppies, ultimately for heroin refining, in the hills surrounding Long Cheng, the Meo-CIA mountain base.

Occasionally, some segments of the Meo tribespeople do not wish to cooperate with the CIA. The CIA has various methods of insuring the loyalty of these mountain tribes. For noncooperating tribespeople there is a terrible price to pay. For example, for six months a segment of Meo tribespeople around Long Pot, eighty miles north of Vientiane, have not been receiving their rice rations. After five years, during which practically no rice has been grown in the region because of the war, the mountain people had become totally dependent upon supplies of rice dropped from American planes. Then suddenly, last February 1971, the planes stopped coming.

Tribal leaders in Long Pot told a visiting American scholar that the rice stopped coming right after the people of the village refused to send their fourteen-year-old youth to fight with the U.S. CIA-financed Meo army of General Vang Pao.

According to Yale instructor Alfred W. McCoy, tribal leaders said Americans from the CIA base at Long Cheng had offered two alternatives for resumption of the relief program: provide more soldiers to General Vang Pao or move their villages within the perimeter of the Long Cheng base complex and participate in poppy farming. The leadership of the recalcitrant tribe refused both alternatives and rice supplies were halted.

The people of Long Pot felt they had given far too much in this war. Almost all of their men fifteen years old and over were already serving with General Vang Pao. "I know the fifteen-year-olds are gone," a chief told McCoy, "because I put them on the helicopter myself."

A move from Long Pot into the CIA base at Long Cheng would make the village totally dependent upon Vang Pao and the Americans, the leaders said. They characterized General Vang Pao as the most hated man in the mountains "for sending the Meo to be killed."

United States AID officials in Vientiane, of course, denied McCoy's charges and insisted that "American policy is to feed any and all refugees." But even an official of the United States-supported regime in Vientiane didn't go along with this. He told McCoy that AID was informed of the Long Pot situation "weeks ago," that they ignored the request for food deliveries, and that the same methods of imposed starvation are being employed against other non-cooperating villages in Laos.

According to a recent report of the U.S. General Accounting Office, "Nearly half of the U.S. AID funds intended to help civilian victims of the war in Laos are being diverted to the CIA's clandestine army. An estimated 2.5 million dollars a year is being diverted from AID public health and food funds to the CIA army." The report further noted that "the CIA and the Defense Department were spending $52.2 million more under the guise of aid to refugees when in fact the money was going to support the para-military forces of General Vang Pao." Senator Kennedy noted that there had been "diversion of the Food for Peace commodities to the military forces which at least violates the spirit of Public Law 480. The decision to involve AID and the Food for Peace program as a cover for support of Lao military forces was made at a high level of the U.S. government. Tens of thousands of Laotian refugees are being pushed around and dying needlessly for our military reasons—under the cover of humanitarian programs."

For those who do cooperate among the Meo tribes, the CIA has taken on the problem of transporting the Meo's *one* commercial crop, opium. Thus the CIA has become a key link in the chain that brings heroin to south * Vietnam and back to the United States.

According to T.D. Allman of the Dispatch News Services: "The CIA helped to consolidate Laotian General

---

* Small "s" is intentional. The 1954 Geneva Accords stipulated that the 17th parallel dividing north and south Vietnam be a *"provisional military* [emphasis added] demarcation line and not a political boundary or national frontier to divide one country into two." Virtually every country of the world, East and West, has abided by those Accords with the exception of the United States.

Vang Pao's lordship of the Meo in the 1960's by using United States and chartered aircraft to transport the Meo opium harvest to market. The CIA also indirectly supported the opium enterprises of the Commander-in-Chief of the Royal Lao Armed Forces, General Ouane Rathikone, a known opium trafficker who has been under surveillance by Interpol for some time. The CIA helped the General because his trade of United States-donated arms for opium with the counterinsurgent tribal groups of Northeast Burma helped keep open the espionage routes to China.

"In southeastern Laos, Prince Soun Oum Long has run a Catch 22 type operation—trading rice and U.S. arms with the Communists while providing men for U.S. operations against the Ho Chi Minh Trail."

The CIA and the U.S. AID Office of Public Safety has conduited hundreds of thousands of dollars to Chao Sopsaisana, vice-president of the Laotian National Assembly, whose recent appointment as ambassador to France was nullified when he showed up at Paris's Orly Airport with a load of heroin in his suitcase.

One United States official commented: "We wanted the territory to use against North Vietnam and the Meo wanted the hills to grow opium. Neither of us had any illusions."

An early 1972 broadcast on KSFX-FM in San Francisco featured a former member of the U.S. Special Forces Team in Laos, Paul F. Withers, who received nine purple hearts during his three years of service in Southeast Asia. Withers said that he actually purchased opium from Meo tribesmen when he worked for the CIA in 1966. Withers further pointed out that he had been assigned by the CIA to work with and to train the Meo tribe members to fight against Communist forces.

Withers noted that while working with the CIA-supported guerrillas, one of his assigned tasks was to notify his contacts by radio when a shipment of opium was ready to be picked up. According to Withers, about every other week the CIA's Air America would land at the small airstrip near where he worked. The tribespeople would unload arms and small bags of gold dust and would exchange these for bags of opium that they had grown. The Air America plane, now loaded with 25 to 100 pounds of raw opium-heroin, would take off "in the direction of south Vietnam."

Withers specifically states that he was instructed to deal for the opium in exchange for the loyalty of the Meo tribespeople, who would then fight for the CIA against the various revolutionary forces in the area.

While Withers admitted that he wasn't certain where the CIA-Air America flights eventually deposited their opium cargo, he did say he was pretty certain that upon his (Withers) return to Saigon, he actually saw some of the Meo's opium—refined down to heroin—being sold in the To Do street market in Saigon. Withers said the heroin in Saigon was in the unique bags identical to those he had seen made by the Meo tribes.

Withers, who is now living in Kansas, said he was extremely fearful of action being taken against him because of his public remarks. He is currently being guarded by Vietnam Veterans Against the War.

In view of the CIA's active involvement in heroin trade, it was perhaps somewhat astonishing to hear presidential candidate Hubert H. Humphrey on January 30, 1972, while speaking at a drug treatment center in Miami, state that "the Central Intelligence Agency should be put to work in the effort to end heroin smuggling." To use Humphrey's old phrase about the Viet Cong's participation in a Vietnamese coalition government: "That's like putting the fox in the coop to guard the chickens."

In the January 30, 1971, issue of the *Far Eastern Economic Review*, Carl Strock reported, "Over the years eight journalists, including myself, have slipped into Long Cheng, the Meo-CIA base, and have seen American crews loading U.S.-supplied T-38 bombers, while armed CIA agents chatted with uniformed Thai soldiers and piles of raw opium stood near-by ready for sale and distribution." This situation was subsequently confirmed by Congressman Robert Steele (D, Conn.), himself a former CIA agent. Steele's report says that the CIA's air cover, i.e., the "Air America" fleet of planes, humorously referred to as "your Terry and the Pirates airline," has been used to transport heroin throughout Southeast Asia. Parenthetically, the report notes, for what it's worth, that the CIA does not have any official policy of letting its planes be used to move the drugs. However, according to the *Christian Science Monitor* of May 29, 1970, ". . . there is evidence that designated opium shipments are cleared and monitored by the CIA on their way out of Laos by air." As David Feingold says, ". . . it can always be argued that anyone who gets at all involved with the political economy of Laos ends up involved with opium. The French, Chinese, and the Vietnamese, north and south; the rightist, the neutralist, and leftist Lao . . . all have traded and fought over opium. Why should it be any different with us?"

Another interesting sidelight is the fact that many of the planes used in moving the drugs were and are manufactured by Lockheed, giving one pause about the intensive efforts put forth in the recent, successful, and even unprecedented lobbying campaign to save Lockheed from bankruptcy.

Exactly how much opium-heroin is being produced in Laos is, of course, virtually impossible to determine. Even during the period of the French opium monopoly at the turn of the century, when considerably less opium was grown, production figures were greatly underestimated. French figures have never been regarded as highly accurate, given the French interest in the heroin trade. In a United Press International dispatch dated as recently as October 17, 1971, it was noted that "The U.S. government estimates that up to 80 percent of the heroin illegally sold in the United States comes through French ports." France's Marseilles continues to be a major refining and disembarkation point for heroin from Southeast Asia on its way to the United States.

On November 26, 1971, French newspapers reported that General Pierre Billotte, a former French minister of defense, had called for the dissolution of the French S.D.E.C.E., France's equivalent to our CIA. General Billotte noted that the S.D.E.C.E. was heavily involved in heroin smuggling both into France and into the United States. To compound matters, the secret French agency was found to be using counterfeit American currency for most of their narcotics transactions.

According to the testimony of former S.D.E.C.E. agent Roger Louette, "French intelligence agents engage in drug smuggling, at least in part, when they need money to finance special assignments." Louette's testimony has been confirmed by Judge Frederick B. Lacey of the U.S. District Court in Newark, N. J.

Not surprisingly, as recently as five years ago the French had only four narcotics agents in all of Marseilles. While the number has just recently been increased to seventy-five, there has been no visible slowing of the heroin flow into the United States. The only visible effect has been the establishment of heroin refining laboratories outside of France—in Brussels, Amsterdam, Madrid, and Zurich.

The French never ratified the Hague International Opium Convention of 1912. In 1924, as L. Roubaud in his book *Vietnam* points out, a French delegate to an international meeting on the control of opium stated, apparently with a straight face, that all of Indochina produced very little opium a year, despite the fact, that as Donald Lancaster notes in his book, *The Emancipation of French Indochina*, the French opium monopoly contributed one-quarter of the revenue for all of Indochina. Perhaps not coincidentally, Laos is the world's highest recipient, on a per capita basis, of United States foreign aid.

Regardless, what is occurring in Laos is occuring in neighboring Thailand, Burma, Cambodia, and Vietnam. An operation of this magnitude must involve, at the very least, the tacit complicity of high governmental officials of all the countries involved, including possibly the United States.

In terms of upper-echelon Vietnamese involvement, in 1971 a member of the U.S. House of Representatives, before the House Foreign Affairs Committee, named a high-ranking south Vietnamese general, Brigadier General Ngo Dzu, as "one of the chief traffickers in heroin in Southeast Asia." General Ngo Dzu's transportation equipment was supplied by United States forces in Vietnam. Testimony at the hearing revealed that since "the General is one of the stauchest military backers of President Thieu and one of the leading strongmen in all of south Vietnam," the United States would be reluctant to take steps against him for fear of disrupting the fragile stability of the Thieu regime.

On September 11, 1971, President Thieu, in spite of the above information being public knowledge, actually promoted Brigadier General Dzu to the rank of lieutenant general.

In July of 1971 President Thieu himself was accused by National Broadcasting Company correspondent Phil Brady of using funds from the illegal opium market to help finance his campaign for reelection in the coming fall. Brady had spent a total of six years in Vietnam. Following the filing of Brady's report, which was backed by NBC administrators, Thieu had Brady disaccredited "for providing help and comfort to the Communist enemy" and subsequently expelled from the country.

Investigative reporter Henry Kamm, following a lengthy stay in Vietnam, reported that despite some United States officials calling for a crackdown on the Vietnamese drug trade, "only token steps have been taken and thus there has been no increase in the retail price of drugs." What pressure Thieu has used, has been to blame and/or arrest his political opponents for the Vietnamese drug traffic.

In *The New York Times* report of these and parallel hearings in the U.S. Senate, Attorney General John W. Mitchell, under intense questioning from Senator Edmund S. Muskie, admitted ". . . that high leaders in Burma, south Vietnam, Laos, and Thailand are deeply involved in heroin traffic."

Later, Senator Charles Mathias, Jr. (R, Md.), at the same hearings, said he presumed that any of these big-league drug traffickers would be ineligible to run in the upcoming election in south Vietnam. Mitchell replied that he couldn't answer the question "and wouldn't if I could in open session."

Richard Kleindienst of ITT fame and now Attorney General was so moved by his then boss's testimony that he exclaimed:

"I believe the record will undisputedly show that John

Mitchell has been the greatest Attorney General that the Department of Justice has had in its history."

In terms of American involvement at mid- or upper-echelon levels, we have at least implicit evidence from the *Chicago Sun-Times,* which reported that on April 25, 1970, an Air Force major and holder of the Air Force Cross was convicted of transporting nine hundred pounds of heroin from Thailand. Not completely surprising is the fact that the major had served as the personal pilot for both the United States Ambassador to south Vietnam, Ellsworth Bunker, and for General William Westmoreland, commander of all United States forces in Vietnam.

If one of the reasons for these Southeast Asian countries' heavy involvement in the heroin trade is the CIA's support for counterinsurgent, opium-growing tribes in those countries, then a second reason is the immediate geographic presence of the vast American market for heroin, namely United States troops in Vietnam, as well as in Thailand, Korea, and Formosa. As Congressman Steele says, as reported in the *New York Post* of May 5, 1971, "Throughout Laos the heroin operation is protected and abetted by Prince Boun Oun, Inspector-General of the realm. The Prince gets his share of the profits from the drug running operation. Once processed, the heroin is flown in to south Vietnam aboard military and occasionally civilian aircraft supplied by various U.S. agencies." The *Christian Science Monitor* points out, among other things in its May 29, 1970, review on heroin, that both the Laotian Army and Air Force are active participants in the heroin trade and that Laotian planes spend a substantial part of their time moving the drug around. Congressman Steele says that "Some of the carefully wrapped packages of the white powder (heroin) are air dropped near U.S. troop emplacements in the fields. Other supplies of heroin reach the troops after being landed at outlying air strips or flown directly into Saigon's Tansonhut airport," where former Vice-President Ky has his home. Somewhat expectantly the March 22, 1971, issue of the *New York Post* cited a letter from a former CIA employee, S.M. Mustard, who charged that former Vice-President Ky himself had once flown opium out of Laos. In April of 1968 a U.S. Senate Subcommittee on Foreign Aid Expenditures issued a report which accused Vice-President Ky, while under the employ of the CIA, of having been active in flying opium from Laos to Saigon. The CIA, while not specifically objecting to his activities, was nevertheless perturbed that these opium-running activities consumed so much of Ky's time. Thus the CIA decided they could get more for their money and discharged Ky from the Agency's employ.

The use of aircraft in the heroin trade on a large-scale basis is an important modern addition, which did not really begin until the United States became involved in Southeast Asia.

As Peter Dale Scott, professor at the University of California at Berkeley and author of *The Politics of Escalation in Vietnam*, points out, one of the more interesting of the CIA's Air America (formerly Civil Air Transport-CAT, Inc.) activities was its supply of arms to the Kuomintang Nationalist Chinese troops (KMT) who didn't go to Formosa but stayed behind in Burma and Thailand to continue fighting against the People's Republic of China. The Nationalist's leader, "General Li Mi is probably the only major opium-dealer in the world to have been honored with the U.S. Legion of Merit and the U.S. Medal of Freedom." When the Burmese government asked the United States to get the Chinese Nationalist troops out of their country, the CIA-CAT was called upon for transportation. Because the Nationalist troops (KMT) refused to move and because "the CIA saw these troops as a thorn in Mao's side, the CIA-CAT continued to supply the KMT with arms and money even though they had decided to settle down and become rich by growing opium." The KMT troops were also helpful to the CIA in organizing and supporting anti-Communist counterinsurgencies throughout a large area of Indochina, particularly through their influence with numerous anti-Communist Chinese communities and secret societies in Southeast Asia. One of these secret societies, the Hip Sings, with branches in the United States, lost its national president, Yee On Li, when he was convicted in the United States for a narcotics operation involving Lucky Luciano's partner. Scott believes that the CIA-CAT-KMT opium-smuggling operations have provided funding for Chiang Kai-Shek's China Lobby in the U.S. Congress. Chiang, of course, was one of the founders of the Kuomintang (KMT).

Professor Ross Y. Koen in his 1960 book, *The China Lobby in American Politics*, wrote: "There is considerable evidence that a number of Nationalist Chinese officials engaged in the illegal smuggling of narcotics into the U.S. with the full knowledge and connivance of the Nationalist Chinese Government. The evidence indicates that several prominent Americans have participated in and profited from these transactions. It indicates further that the narcotics business has been an important factor in the activities and permutations of the China Lobby."

Of historical interest is the fact that much of President Nixon's early financial support for his congressional campaigns came from the China Lobby, at least in part, because of his vehement anti-Communist, pro-Chinese Nationalist stance. Perhaps then it should not surprise us that Nixon will proclaim that "narcotics addiction is spreading with pandemic virulence" and that "what is needed is an integrated attack . . . on the movement of narcotics across international borders, *particularly Turkey and France*," [emphasis added] when in fact the main international borders crossed for opium-heroin distribution are in Laos and Burma and Thailand, areas controlled by KMT troops financed by the China Lobby.

Not surprisingly, a recent issue of *U.S. News and World Report* notes that "In all areas of the antidrug drive, President Nixon has assumed direct responsibility," thereby emphasizing Turkey and France and not Southeast Asia.

Among the more prominent members of the China Lobby are:

Ray Cline, Chief of Intelligence for the State Department.

Anna Chennault (Her husband was one of the founders of "Air America.")

As had been J. Edgar Hoover, FBI director.

While the CIA has its corporate fronts such as CAT and later Air America, Inc., it may be instructive to note that the parent company of Air America, Inc., is the Pacific Corporation. If Air America directs heroin traffic, it is both informative and ironic that the following men are on the Board of Directors of the Pacific Corporation, which in turn directs Air America:

SAMUEL RANDOLPH WALKER, director, Equitable Life Assurance Society; life trustee, Columbia University; member, Action Council for Better Cities.

WILLIAM GARRARD REED, director, Boeing Aircraft Co.; director, Northern Pacific Railroad; director, Stanford University Research Institute.

ARTHUR BERRY RICHARDSON, director, Chesebrough-Ponds, Inc.; director, Lenox Hill Hospital; director, United Hospital Fund of New York City; officer, State Department, "China desk," 1914–1936.

JAMES BARR AMES, director, United Community Service; director, Animal Rescue League; trustee, Mt. Auburn Hospital; director, Air Asia Co. (subsidiary of Air America).
CHARLES P. CABELL, retired general; deputy director, CIA (1953–1962).

It may seem too absurd to even imagine, but can a director of the Animal Rescue League or a director of the United Hospital Fund or a member of the Action Council for Better Cities be some of the biggest pushers in the world? Perhaps they can if one also realizes that they are also major stockholders in and/or directors of defense industries (e.g., Reed, Walker, and Ames) and/or held important political positions in Southeast Asian counterinsurgency programs (e.g., Richardson and Cabell).

Scott summarizes the situation: "The apparent involvement of CIA proprietaries [e.g., CAT-Air America] with foreign narcotics operations is paralleled by their apparent interlock with the domestic institutions involved with organized crime. The need to understand such involvements more fully may well become more urgent in the future, as the Indochina war is 'Vietnamized' and handed over increasingly to CIA proprietaries. Wealthy U.S. interests using the secret authorities delegated to the CIA have resorted systematically to organized outlaws to pursue their operations. The opium based economy of Laos is being protected by a coalition of opium growing CIA mercenaries, Air America planes and Thai troops. The recent attempts at crackdowns on Turkish opium production can only increase the importance of Indochinese opium."

There can be little doubt that the various wars waging throughout most of Southeast Asia have disrupted conventional land distribution routes of opium-heroin, thus leaving the distributors more dependent upon U.S.-supplied aircraft and monitoring of air lanes. Air transportation avoids the headaches and costs of ground transportation and thus increases profit margins. Air transportation is particularly relevant from an agricultural perspective as well. Namely, a greater concentration of quality opium can be harvested at higher altitudes, and still reach foreign markets. Steep mountain trails would make the opium growers' access to the market limited, were it not for the specialized aircraft supplied by the United States, for example, helicopters and short-takeoff and landing (STOL) aircraft.

Moreover, as a case in point, in Thailand, where heroin offenses carry the death penalty, the Thai government has nevertheless taken the view that the economy of its tribes on the *upper* reaches of the mountain slopes are so dependent on the growing of opium for heroin that the government will not suppress these mountain crops until a suitable cash crop, which will bring an equivalent profit, can be found to replace it. Of course, there are few cash crops as profitable as opium. Therefore, as David Feingold notes, ". . . the bulk of police activities have been directed against the lowland traders. The Thai case points up an important feature of the heroin trade, also characteristic of the situation in Laos: separation of the highland and lowland trades."

If the "domino theory" is a valid one, where the fall of one country is predicated on the fall of the country adjacent to it, then in Southeast Asia the dominoes are held together by dope. Virtually all the antiguerrilla, pro-American forces in Southeast Asia are, in one way or another, a part of the American heroin empire. Thus attempts at stopping the heroin traffic at its initial sources seems unlikely without a political-military upheaval in these countries, including possibly our own.

As David Feingold says: "In the politics of Laos, Burma, Thailand and Vietnam, the influence of heroin and the billions of dollars involved in its multinational trade (3 billion per year, according to *Business Week*; other estimates range as high as 20 billion per year) are never very far below the surface. Bizarre military strategies, surprising political alliances and 'irrational' policies often become astonishingly comprehensible when examined in terms of the economics and logistics of heroin." For example, since the Geneva Accords, the military confrontations in Laos have tended to be synchronized with the opium agricultural cycle. As H. Toye in *Laos: Buffer State or Battleground* has found: "Throughout the mid-1950's the Pathet Lao controlled the important opium growing regions of Sam Neua and Phong Saly. Following the re-establishment of Royal Laotian Government authority in 1958, conflict broke out again in July, 1959, in time for the Royal Laotian Government to seize the opium that had been collected in the tribal villages." Unfortunately, little of this information reaches the general public. Fear of causing embarrassment to well-placed and U.S.-supported government officials has prevented a full discussion of what should be publicized.

The Committee of Concerned Asian Scholars concludes: "American authorities have effectively used opium-heroin profits to reward Asian elites for their support of U.S. military goals in Southeast Asia. Our government not only supplies arms and aid to the protectors of the heroin trade, but it also supplies a captive body of consumers—over 200,000 GI's in Indochina. The bankrupt policies of counterrevolution abroad and 'benign neglect' at home promote heroin addiction."

The third geopolitical reason for a continuing heavy concentration of opium growth in Southeast Asia is the expanding market that nearby Japan represents. Japan has become a miniaturized United States, even in its consumption of heroin. As recently as August 1971, *The New York Times* reported that an American Air Force captain, who was also a medical officer and physician, was arrested in Tokyo, along with two military associates, for distributing heroin, not only to Americans based in Japan, but also to a growing Japanese heroin addict population, at least in part created by the American presence in Japan.

Given the market for heroin in Vietnam by United States troops, in Japan by the Japanese and again by United States troops stationed there, and in the United States itself, there has been a considerable economic incentive for increased heroin production in Indochina. The market has expanded to the point where one can become an "addict gourmet" and flavor the various "name brands" now on the market, such as "999 brick," "Yunnan opium," "red rock," "No. 3 purple smoking heroin" and "No. 4 white heroin."

3 How Heroin Comes
to America

There have been some attempts by various United States agencies to suppress heroin at its agricultural origins. These plans work along the same lines as do our price-parity and price-support programs for American farmers. Basically, the United States is offering poppy-growing farmers money, in exchange for their not growing or for turning in to the government their poppy crop, from which the opium and heroin are derived. There are a number of problems with this price-support program. First of all, the program has been primarily carried out in Middle East countries, such as Turkey, which are no longer the prime sources of American heroin.

Second is the fact that the price-support program was to end Turkish poppy growth by 1972. Unfortunately, the Turkish government has just issued a hundred and fifty thousand poppy-growing licenses, almost double the number for 1971, which produced the biggest poppy crop in Turkish history. The crop was so large that a reporter for *Newsweek* estimated that it would produce enough illegal opium to keep heroin factories in business for years, even in the unlikely event of Turkey's stopping its poppy growth.

And worse, the end does not seem in sight. New York Congressman Seymour Halpern has noted that the Turks expect to issue up to three hundred thousand poppy-growing licenses the following year. The Turkish government claims the program is a great success, stating that they were able to collect 149 tons of opium in 1971, compared to only 60 tons the previous year. What the government isn't noting is the fact that as more and more opium is grown by more and more farmers, it becomes an increasingly simple task to divert any "surplus" crop to the profitable black market.

New York State Senator John H. Hughes points out that there are at least sixty thousand Turkish poppy farmers. If each holds out only four to five pounds of poppy from his 1971 and 1972 crops, "there will be enough to supply the American heroin market for most of the decade."

A somewhat similar set of circumstances is occurring in France, where according to an Associated Press report, "The French Government is *encouraging* the growth of opium poppies, insisting that the product will be used only for medicinal purposes." Needless to say, it will require only a minimal amount of illegal skimming to provide supplies of raw opium for the American heroin market. Halpern concluded about the poppy-purchase program that "our State Department appears once again to have been the victim of an end run." Cynicism is so pervasive about the ineffectiveness of stopping poppy farming in the Middle East that it's increasingly called the "Cold Turkey Plan." Others simply say, "poppy-crop."

In spite of the lack of success of this program, the United States is giving Turkey over 200 million dollars a year to support it directly and indirectly. And to make matters worse, a Turkish cabinet minister asserted that far more money will be demanded. *The New York Times* called it "a shameful exercise, reminding one of the tribute demanded by the Barbary pirates in the early eighteen hundreds. For the U.S. to pay tribute to a 'friend' for the dubious honor of not adding to our national sickness must surely be a laughing matter for our friends and enemies alike. When we allow drug pushers to walk our streets, thanks to the venality of our police officials . . . we can hardly expect cooperative action from the Turks."

The third problem with the agricultural price-support-suppression approach is the fact that 99 percent of all opium growth in the Middle East is legitimate and the opium growth used for legal medicinal purposes such as codeine, a well-known and often used prescription analgesic (i.e., pain killer). In addition, the Ford Foundation addiction research team has calculated that only about thirty-five hundred acres or five square miles of poppy growth are necessary in order to supply the entire American heroin market every year. Since this is such a relatively tiny area, numerous poppy farms can and do operate clandestinely and profitably without fear of detection or prosecution.

Ultimately, agricultural suppression of opium-heroin by a price-support program in one country simply encourages and insures its growth in another country, given the huge profits available for poppy growth. After all, the poppy can be grown in all the continents of the world with the exception of Antarctica, and even there a greenhouse operation might be profitable enough for consideration.

Interestingly enough, while the United States official position on heroin is one of total suppression, the United States has done very little to suppress it at its source. For example, the United States has in its possession numerous chemical defoliants that could be used to destroy any poppy-opium growth. While these same defoliants have been used to destroy the Viet Cong's forest hideouts, they have not been used to destroy the neighboring visible and often massive opium farm plots.

Former Marine colonel and Presidential Crime Commissioner Dr. William R. Corson suggests that we go even further. He suggests that we consider heroin addiction to be the "result of an aggression against the people of the United States, in substance no different from that of Hitler's against the Jews, that is, a form of genocide, and that we destroy poppy plants where they are found." Corson notes that "such an action has ample recent precedent. After all, if President Nixon is able to justify our invasion of Cambodia as a 'preventative aggression,' why not—for starters—use our air power to napalm the poppy fields in Laos and Cambodia, which would, incidentally, render those fields incapable of producing opium for at least five years." In view of the fact that the United States has routinely napalmed whole villages of women and children throughout Southeast Asia, it hardly seems extreme to napalm poppy plants. Corson concludes: "The prospect of even sterner measures to enable the American people to maintain their rights of self-determination, which are clearly threatened by heroin, should not be ruled out merely because the heroin aggressors are our government's allies."

Unfortunately, the United States seems to be denying or avoiding or hiding, even, the information that heroin comes from Indochina in general and from Laos in particular. For example, in the U.S. Government Printing Office's publications on Laos, of the 349 pages of political, social, and economic data presented, only three sentences are devoted to opium—the first of which is historical, the last, noting that "this form of trade has virtually ceased."

Heroin is so simple to grow, so compact in its growth, so easy to handle and transport, that arrests of American distributors, when they do occur, have been totally ineffectual in cutting down the heroin market supply, even when large amounts of heroin have been seized. The accessibility to the foreign sources of heroin is so great that the Ford Foundation investigators report that the Mafia and other major distributors have upwards of a ten-year supply of heroin on hand as insurance against one of their sources being eliminated.

The U.S. Attorney for the Southern District of New York has pointed out that during a recent five-month period, the government has stopped more heroin from coming into this country than at any period in United States history. He noted that "these seizures, amounting to more than half a ton of undiluted heroin, represent a diversion of black market drugs having a retail value on the street of more than $100 million dollars. According to federal authorities, the seizures represent nearly 10 percent of the annual supply of illegal heroin coming into the U.S. This is law enforcement at its finest, with brilliant investigative work, effective legal steps, and international cooperation of the highest order. And yet, as the dust has settled, the impact on the street supply and the price of heroin is virtually unchanged. The most dramatic professional law enforcement measures are not enough to cut off the supply of heroin."

Following other recent, large seizures of heroin, the U.S. Attorney for the Southern District of New York said that ". . . law enforcement efforts have not made the slightest ripple in the heroin supply . . . the suppliers are able to meet the demand regardless of what we do on the law

enforcement part." One of the reasons for the ineffectiveness of law enforcement techniques is organized crime's
use of what is called the "shotgun approach" to smuggling
heroin into New York City, for example. According to
William J. Durkin, the regional director of the U.S. Bureau
of Narcotics and Dangerous Drugs, "The Mafia drug ring
would hire in Europe four or five couriers at a time, conceal 5 to 10 pounds of heroin in secret compartments of
their luggage or on their persons and send them to New
York through varying routes. If a courier or his or her luggage was caught at customs, the loss of heroin was small
and the bulk of the shipment always got through. . . . On
one day in 1968, for example, a French courier named
Joseph Cartier was caught at Kennedy Airport with a
pouch containing six pounds of heroin strapped around his
leg; however, four other couriers entered the country at
different points undetected."

Dr. William Corson delineates some of the heroin smuggling techniques that are virtually uncontrollable by any
law enforcement agencies:

"For example, it has been known for many years that
much of the heroin which enters the United States from
the Far East does so on U.S. Navy ships. The basic method
is simple. It involves hiding a 'loaf' or package aboard a
ship visiting a Far Eastern port. The heroin dealers will
hire, coerce, bribe, or otherwise intimidate a sailor to 'just
pick up a package for us when you arrive in Hong Kong,
the Philippines, Tokyo, etc., and hide it aboard ship.' Payment varies, but the point is impressed on those who accept the deal that to try and go into business for themselves with the 'package' would be extremely bad for their
health. Then when the ship reaches the port the sailor is
expected to go to a designated dance hall, tailor's, curio
shop, etc., identify himself by a prearranged code and pick

up the heroin (which may be hidden in anything from a stereo tape recorder to the lining of an overcoat). Once back aboard ship he is required to hide the heroin according to instructions, e.g., 'ventilator shaft No. 123 in a steel box welded two feet to the right behind access plate 12.'

"From the moment the heroin is hidden aboard, the likelihood of preventing the entry of the heroin into the United States is virtually nil. The ship returns home, goes to a shipyard, workers come aboard to repair and prepare the ship for its next voyage. Among the workers there is one who knows about access plate 12. He opens it, takes the heroin off the ship, and delivers it to dealers. Throughout this entire process no search is practicable; in foreign ports there are just too many people, both Navy and indigenous people, going aboard ship, for proper searches in the time available, quite apart from the question of who is to search the searchers. Aboard a U.S. aircraft carrier there are more places and more ways to hide ten million dollars worth of heroin than in a medium-sized city."

As mentioned previously, the advent of the airplane has altered narcotics traffic, making law enforcement even more difficult. When the East Coast is tied up, as it was with a recent fifty-nine-day dock strike, or is being watched especially closely, the Mexican border can be an inviting port of entry, particularly by air. According to Robert Lindsey of *The New York Times* (November 30, 1971), "along the sparsely settled frontier that divides the U.S. and Mexico, air-borne drug runners are doing a booming business, and federal agents say they do not know how to stop them. On most nights, agents estimate, at least ten planes cross the border with drugs." By flying low and slow and landing in sagebrush-covered desert, they are virtually undetectable by radar and officials' planes.

Donald A. Quick, a U.S. Customs agent, notes: "Anybody who knows how to fly can get into the business and make a lot of money in a hurry and get away with it. You get bush pilots, soldiers of fortune and guys who flew with the CIA in Vietnam, and a lot of 'em can't get jobs. Pilots are a dime a dozen these days and they're willing to do anything to fly, including drug smuggling."

An official of the Justice Department stated: "They're developing their own air force, and its getting bigger and bigger. Some pilots are using DC-3 Constellations which can carry 40,000 pounds of drugs." This is a particularly ominous sign since the entire U.S. heroin market consumes less than seventy thouand pounds of heroin a year. Therefore, two heroin-filled flights by a DC-3 would be sufficient to supply the U.S. heroin market for an entire year. Obviously, with the more than a few planes and pilots available, it has become ridiculously simple to accumulate vast reserves of heroin. In fact, the heroin reserves are becoming so great that the Ford Foundation has reported that the street-level cost of heroin is actually decreasing in some places as the supply exceeds the demand.

United States agents in an attempt to stop the flow and flight of heroin into the United States have purchased thirty unmarked helicopters, but when they must cover a border of over fifteen hundred miles, up to an altitude of eighteen thousand feet twenty-four hours a day, and where radar is ineffective below nine thousand feet, successful surveillance becomes improbable.

However, with a lot of federal law enforcement subsidies available, Defense Department contractors are increasingly interested in becoming Justice Department contractors without doing any additional research on their technology. For example, Robert Barkan, a former senior engineer at the Electronic Defense Laboratories of the

Sylvania Electronic Systems, reports that while Nixon
Vietnamizes the war in Southeast Asia he is quietly "Amer-
icanizing" the war's technology in the United States.
Barkan notes that dope "smugglers on the U.S.-Mexican
border face a new obstacle to their trade. The U.S. Border
Patrol is now flying Air Force 'Pave Eagle' airplanes un-
manned, remote controlled drones—formerly used in the
billion dollar Igloo White anti-infiltration program in Laos.
Flying over remote stretches of the border, the planes re-
lay signals from hundreds of ground sensors to an 'Infiltration Surveillance Center,' where huge computers diagnose
the data. But as in Vietnam, the sophisticated electronic
systems cannot quite distinguish 'friend' from 'foe.' A wan-
dering burro or a traveling hippie can send the border
patrolmen scrambling for their jeeps—and guns.

"Ground sensors currently experimented with on the
Mexican border are adaptations of the devices used to
detect the sounds and vibrations of the movements of
troops and supply trucks on the Ho Chi Minh Trail. Their
use on the Mexican border is reportedly a result of Attorney General John Mitchell's 'interest in surveillance discoveries and techniques.' The sensors were deployed in the
summer of 1970, when the Border Patrol, an arm of the
Justice Department, received a proposal for the sensor surveillance system from Sylvania Electronics, which had
produced sensors for use in Indochina." Sylvania noted
that "The political implications of using surveillance equipment along a friendly foreign border have been considered
by selecting equipment that can be deployed without at-
tracting attention and easily concealed."

In a recent Associated Press report entitled "Spaced-
Out," it was noted that federal government narcs will be
even tougher to spot. The Bureau of Narcotics has begun
work on a satellite that would be able to detect opium-

poppy fields from a distance of one hundred miles above the ground. At present the Bureau is giving $2 million to military contractors in an attempt to determine the "signature" of opium. The "signature" is the pattern by which a plant reflects heat and light during various phases of growth. However, Dr. Robert Miller of the U.S. Department of Agriculture notes that the system will not be perfect "because even with an established signature we won't be able to detect relatively small crops"—and it takes only a small crop of poppy to be profitable.

One of the more esoteric surveillance devices has recently been developed by the RPC Corporation of El Segundo, California, which usually confines its work to military contracts. This time, New York City, with the help of Justice Department funding, has paid for the development of a "bioluminescent heroin sniffer." The device makes use of plankton, odor sensitive to heroin. According to writer Mary Breasted, "Although the exact function of the plankton is apparently classified, they apparently give off certain electrical signals when they smell heroin." An RPC official, when questioned as to how far away it works, responded, "It depends upon how much heroin you have; it's only in the development phase."

The Electronics Industries Association, composed primarily of Defense Department contractors, has estimated that the annual market in antidrug law enforcement electronics begins at $400 million annually with the likelihood for vast increases.

Barkan reports that a government official told engineers at a 1969 industrial conference: "Generally, no legal limitations on electronic surveillance of large public areas exist." He added: "the challenge is wide open. There is a great unrestricted area of electronic surveillance and electronic countercrime measures in which there needs to be expansion and further innovation."

Paul Baran, an engineer with the Rand Corporation, warned in 1967 that by permitting the unrestricted adoption of sophisticated technology by the police, "we could easily end up with the most effective, oppressive police state ever created."

Baran observed that "there is an unmistaken amorality which infects some of my engineering colleagues. That is, whatever we are paid to work on we automatically rationalize to be a blessing to mankind. . . . Too many of my brethren think that merely because something can be built and sold, it should be." With unemployment among their colleagues at an all-time high, engineers are further motivated to work on anything they can get paid for.

"Their corporate employers, faced with dwindling federal funds for aerospace and defense, are eagerly looking for new markets. Surveillance equipment for the home drug front is a particularly easy transfer and expansion of Vietnam technology."

In Indochina or along the Mexican border, the electronic battlefield components industry is virtually recession proof. Even if the public finds the war in Vietnam more and more distasteful, the public concern in general over "law and order," and in particular over drugs, is growing. The Justice Department is "visibly" responding by purchasing more and more electronic hardware. If the public finds Defense research and development (R & D) too repugnant, the Defense R & D may surrpetitiously be carried on as "antinarcotics research" where "junkies" are the enemy, instead of "gooks."

Moreover, the hundreds of millions of federal dollars earmaked for law-and-order technology dwarf the few millions available for such needs as environmental pollution control. To industry the choice is clear. The extent of its concern for the way technology can best serve humanity was succinctly expressed a few years ago by a vice-president of the giant Avco Corporation: "We have a modest amount of altruism and a lot of interest in profits."

In spite of the new technology, and because of the potential for easy success and quick profits—for example, ten *ounces* of heroin purchased in Mexico for $3,500 can be sold the same day in Los Angeles for $140,000—more and more pilots are lured into the drug-smuggling business. The Arizona State Department of Public Safety says: "We know of approximately ten different organized operations in Tucson alone, each involving six to eight people, that are flying in loads weekly." Not surprisingly, customs agents recently arrested the city attorney of Winslow, Arizona, a town near the border, and accused him of directing a large aerial drug-smuggling operation.

If this level of profit isn't sufficiently attractive, there are other factors which make the aerial smuggling even more alluring, namely, product diversification. As a *New York Times* study points out, the smugglers, often referred to as "contrabandistas," operate from small airports along the American side of the border, flying U.S. merchandise such as refrigerators, televisions, and tobacco into Mexico and Central and South America without paying import duties. Actually, as far as U.S. Customs is concerned, such flights are legal as long as readily available export permits are obtained. South of the border, the "contrabandistas" usually bribe local officials and earn a solid profit by selling their duty-free merchandise. Then they go to a regional heroin distributor for a heroin supply for the return flight north. In this way, with the addition of the southbound flight full of refrigerators, etc., they make a profit going both ways, saving time and making more money, with little added risk.

For airborne smugglers on a North-South route, Florida has increasingly assumed a major role for heroin transporters. Southern Florida has sixty scattered small airfields. Many of these fields have no control towers, no paving, and *no customs procedures*. Custom officials have pointed out that one smuggling team used two twin-engined planes with identical markings to ensure a "clean" flight log and cargo load, which allowed heroin to be imported from the Caribbean without custom's clearance, as if it had been on a domestic journey.

Also in Florida, smugglers have been using small boats to supplement air smuggling, using the boats to bring drugs into the many small harbors that dot the Florida coast. Customs officials point out that there are two hundred forty thousand boats registered in the state, an impossible number to keep under surveillance.

With the growing success of heroin smuggling, Latin America is an increasingly attractive heroin distribution point, prior to entry into the United States. The director of the Federal Bureau of Narcotics, upon his recent return from Latin America, said: "Latin America is now up to its ears in heroin." The Bureau noted that it has become particularly interested in Panama for the following reasons.

1. Pilots are not only carrying processed heroin from France to Panama (and ultimately to the United States), but are also transporting cocaine, which flourishes in the countries surrounding Panama.

2. With fifteen seaports and over a hundred known airfields, surveillance in Panama is exceptionally difficult. Among Panamanians arrested this year in connection with

drug seizures was the chief of air traffic control at Tocamen Airport in Panama.

The Bureau stated: "It is clear that the Republic of Panama has not and is not paying sufficient attention to narcotic enforcement activities to achieve any noticeable results. This may be due to apathy and/or collusion."

In support of these charges, on March 15, 1972, Congressman John Murphy stated that "heroin smuggling into the United States had touched the highest levels of the Government of Panama, including Juan Tack, foreign minister, and Moises Torrijos, Panama's ambassador to Spain, and more importantly the brother of General Omar Torrijos, ruler of Panama." Perhaps relevantly, General Torrijos received his military training at various mainland U.S. military installations.

What is of particular significance about Panama is its parallels and analogies to the heroin trade occurring in Southeast Asia: Panama, like Vietnam or Thailand, is a country where large numbers of U.S. servicemen are stationed, and like Indochina it is a focal point, or at least an important staging area, for further heroin distribution.

As the North American Congress on Latin America points out: "Strategically, the Canal area is the door to Latin America, in much the same way that Vietnam is to Southeast Asia, and as such it has become a center for U.S. military and economic control of the entire hemisphere. The Canal area houses the infamous counterinsurgency, counterguerrilla training school where U.S. experts instruct Latin American military men in the latest methods of repressing revolutionary movements within their respective countries, again as is done in Vietnam.

"Over the past decade within Panama itself there has been a broad-based effort to eliminate U.S. control of the area. As early as 1964 there was a large student demonstration during which the U.S. flag over the Canal was torn down. The demonstrators were met by U.S. military men who killed 27 people and injured over 700.

"Since that time, as in Vietnam, the U.S. has relied heavily on CIA activities to try to gain control of the situation. Since that time Panama's importance as a center of heroin distribution has increased. The walls of many of Panama's buildings are painted with 'Viva la DemocraCIA.'"

Suppression of heroin smuggling at one border simply insures delivery at another border. Suppression of a particular means or methods of smuggling heroin simply insures the development of new smuggling means and technology, ranging from airplanes to pliable plastic pouches that can hold a few, but profitable, pounds of heroin and yet be small enough to insert into a woman's vagina. And even should these methods fail, and in general they haven't, officials can always be bribed.

To stretch possibilities to an extreme, what would happen if it were possible to suppress totally all aspects of heroin smuggling? Given the fact that the conditions that breed the demand for heroin, namely, poverty, racism, and alienation will continue to flourish, we can be assured that a heroin substitute will be found. Criminally financed laboratories will research and develop an even more highly addicting and euphoric producing drug that can be cheaply synthesized within the borders of the United States by decentralized laboratories throughout the country, thereby obviating any smuggling problems (e.g., *injectible* methadone made in U.S. criminal labs).

Thus, ultimately the control of heroin is not the solution to problems created by an isolated drug, e.g., heroin. There simply are no limits to the number of new and attractive drugs that can be synthetically created or are even naturally available.

Author and drug researcher Alan Watts notes that a group of young people started the great banana hoax a few years ago, stating that one could get high on banana peels. "But nobody in government seems to have gotten the point of the hoax. The people who started this yarn were trying to teach us something and we don't appear to have learned. The lesson is that there are vast numbers of natural and synthetic psychedelics and euphorics and the government is going to look increasingly foolish if it tries to make them all illegal. The nation's leading manufacturer of catnip, which is a mild psychedelic, reports that its sales doubled in 1968—while the cat population remained relatively constant. If catnip were banned, another legal psychedelic or euphoric would become popular. The Swedes have a psychedelic seaweed, and somebody will begin importing it soon, I'm sure—if they haven't already. The government's position against consciousness-expanding and euphoric agents will grow increasingly ridiculous and repressive."

The repressive aspects of the drug laws is called "deliberate" by author and former heroin addict William S. Burroughs, especially since the laws really affect only small-time, personal users of the drugs. Burroughs says alleged "drug control is a thin pretext, and getting thinner, to increase police powers and to brand dissent as criminal. To classify all opposition as criminal—and since most of the opposition, at least at some point, uses illegal drugs from the youth culture using marijuana, from the blacks using heroin, to factory workers and housewives using amphetamines—is, of course, a simple device by which a fascist regime takes over a country."

Aside from even the repressive aspects of the addiction laws there is another angle to consider. At the December 1971 meeting of the American Association for the Ad-

vancement of Science, the largest scientific organization
in the country, numerous papers were presented indicat-
ing that increasing the penalties for the personal use of
heroin actually *increased* the crime rate associated with
addiction.

Watts went on to say: "Possession of *any* drug shouldn't
be a crime. The effect of making simple possession into a
felony is that an agent of the government can place on or
near any dissenter an illegal drug and then make an anonymous phone call to the police."

The problems and issues of drugs are, of course,
much broader than the drugs themselves, but rather have
to do with who and how a society wishes to make policy
about pain and pleasure, poverty and racism.

With only a relatively few acres required to grow a very
profitable crop, air and ground surveillances, payoffs and
farm price supports cannot begin to control heroin traffic,
even if the government were totally dedicated to its removal.

4 Junk Corrupts

What, then, about control of heroin at the national level, within the borders of the United States? Again, profits rear their ugly head. As an example of the profitability of heroin, in 1969, in one area of Laos, prepared opium was selling for four cents per gram. Meanwhile, in New York City it was selling for twenty dollars per gram—a price five hundred times its original value. Such a vast profit margin is bound to attract an unlimited number of people to the American heroin empire's business—regardless of the penalties and risks involved. Profits are so great that corruption of law enforcement officials has become pandemic. In fact, the more officials hired for heroin suppression work, the more are bribed, or worse, become distributors themselves. Thirty federal agents within the last eighteen months alone have been indicted for being directly involved in the heroin (i.e., junk) trade.

The fact is that one of the major reasons for failure of law enforcement methods is that the law enforcers themselves, from the international CIA to local city police, operate outside and against the law, becoming an integral and critical part of the heroin empire. There simply is no good reason to believe that it will be any other way as long as profits from illegal heroin remain so high. In a profit-controlled society, the banker (the fact that he is legal or illegal is irrelevant and only semantic) is king and will call the tune and set the rhythm of the heroin marketplace.

If the situation is bad nationally, it's much worse locally. This book will document a number of cases of flagrant corruption involving many major metropolitan police officials throughout the country, all of whom were or are involved in heroin enterprises. For example, as New York investigative reporter Mary Perot Nichols found: "The Knapp Commission (set up by Mayor Lindsay to investigate police corruption) was cynically thought by some to be avoiding its role when it canceled public hearings last June 1971. However, the fact is that the Commission had gotten hold of something so hot that it had to finish tracking down the leads it uncovered. Where the leads took it was to a group of 35 cops who were actively involved in the heroin business in Harlem. Pictures caught them in the act." Parenthetically, reporter Nichols believed that someone on the Commission informed in advance the Police Commissioner, Patrick Murphy, of the impending bombshell, to which Murphy attempted to respond by firing numerous top level officers.

Commissioner Murphy himself has acknowledged police corruption with regard to heroin. He said on September 19, 1971, that ". . . corruption in narcotics enforcement is there and there is no sense in pretending it's not serious. It's not unusual for an officer in the city to arrest a heroin pusher who has $5,000.00 or $10,000.00 or $15,000.00 cash in his pocket, and the pusher is willing to give it all to the cop to let him go. Sometimes that's the dimension of the corruption problem we have; $10,000.00 can change hands in a few moments."

Unfortunately Commissioner Murphy saw the problem of police corruption as a few rotten apples spoiling an otherwise healthy barrel. Both the Knapp Commission and the New York State Commisison of Investigation have shown that the problem goes considerably beyond the greed of a few isolated cops, and that the "issue is the condition of the barrel itself."

Specifically, the New York State Commission of Investigation, as early as April 22, 1971, considerably before the Knapp Commission, concluded that "the evidence has disclosed beyond question that the overall narcotics law enforcement effort in New York City is a failure." The Commission's ". . . data revealed a startling picture of the futility of narcotics arrests and dispositions both in terms of their quality and their quantity." For example, as Paul H. Curran, chairman of the Commission, pointed out ". . . although police arrest figures for 1968 through 1970 seemed on their face impressive, . . . the vast majority of those arrests involved only misdemeanors for possession of only minute amounts of heroin or hypodermic needles or for loitering for the purpose of personal use of drugs."

Mark Dillen of the University of Michigan commented, "We're in a situation where local law enforcement agencies are carrying on a campaign to 'protect' us, trying to beat to death what is a complex socio-political problem by throwing the greatest victims of hard drug use, the user him/her self, into the most detrimental institutions our society has to offer—our prisons."

As one narcotics agent said, "Even if every street pusher was put behind bars and kept there indefinitely, there would be a whole new team of pushers operating in less than a week. For every pusher on the streets there are four behind him or her in the junkie farm system just waiting for the chance to get someone else to support their habit. There were over 17,000 such misdemeanor arrests in 1968, over 33,000 in 1969 and over 46,000 in 1970." In spite of increasing arrests there was every indication to believe that the addict population was increasing. That, in fact, the increasing number of arrests simply mirrored, in part, the growing addict population, rather than any improvement in law enforcement procedures.

There were similar indications that higher-echelon pushers and distributors were untouched by increasing arrests or convictions and that indeed they seem to be getting away with more than ever. For example, as Curran writes in the *New York Law Journal*: "In 1968 in the entire City of New York only 40 narcotic felony defendants were convicted and in 1969, despite the fact that there were substantially more felony cases reported, only thirty-two felony defendants were convicted. In short, the statistics standing alone established that narcotic enforcement in New York City, as practiced by the police and prosecutors, was little more than a numbers game involving an extremely high volume of arrests of low-echelon violators . . ." and a low volume of arrests for high-echelon violators.

Curran notes that "due to the tremendous volume and low-level kinds of cases that were generally being presented to them, the prosecutors were unable to give narcotics enforcement the kind of attention it deserved."

Approximately one-third of the felony indictments filed in 1970 in New York City involved narcotics crimes, as did 60 percent of misdemeanor cases. In both the overwhelming majority of felony and misdemeanor cases the defendants were poor and more often than not could not make bail, thus filling our prisons way beyond 100 percent of their planned capacity and setting the stage for explosive riots and massacres. As one lawyer said, if it weren't for the permissiveness of some judges who allow plea bargaining, where "we trade years in jail for days in court" and the ability of other judges "to hear three cases at one time, both the Tombs and Attica would have blown five years ago." Of course, if possession of small amounts of heroin were not a crime, our prisons would be substantially less filled and less explosive.

The State Investigation Commission said that "arrests of street-level drug addicts were a waste of time, money, and manpower," not to mention the fact that with so many addicts in our jails and prisons, these institutions have become major breeding grounds for additional addicts. One Detroit prisoner said he was taught in prison to shoot up, "not with a syringe but with a needle on a haircream container. You know, a tube with the end cut off and a point melted into it."

Curran notes that "basic responsibility for narcotics enforcement in New York City lies with the narcotics division of the New York City Police Department. In 1970 this division consisted of approximately 780 police officers of whom 80 were assigned to the special investigations unit, which is responsible for apprehending narcotics violators. The rest of the division consisted of field teams engaged in what might be termed 'street' narcotics enforcement."

A number of present and former members of the narcotics division testified before the Commission that there was a quota system in busy addiction sectors of four felony arrests per month. The police officers testified that "the sole enforcement criterion was arrests, without regard to what kinds of cases were made and without any regard to whether or not arrests resulted in convictions. If an officer did not make his monthly arrest quota, he was threatened with transfer out of the narcotics division," which was certainly undesirable to the officer, given the additional money an officer could make through bribes and payoffs while in the division. Needless to say the setting of quotas and control of assignments and transfers were determined by upper-echelon officers and not by a "few rotten apples" at the bottom of the barrel. And the quota system is hardly unique to New York City.

Commission Chairman Curran says that "this quota system meant that the narcotics division's almost total emphasis was on number of arrests (the numbers game). This in turn meant that the lowest echelon narcotics violators, the street addicts, were the focus of police activity and arrest. Obviously, a police officer could not afford to take the time to make the more difficult higher-level case because if he did so he would be unable to meet his quota. As a direct result of this numbers game approach, the more substantial heroin traffickers have been able to operate with little fear of detection, arrest or conviction."

Former New York City Police Inspector William P. Brown added that "no one has even given a very convincing argument for arresting heroin users, other than that sometimes they can be made to supply information. Certainly, we don't rehabilitate them, and arresting them has done very little indeed to cleanse a community of narcotics."

Brown points out that even those arrests of so-called middle- and higher-echelon dealers often turn out to be very small-time dealers known as "accommodation" or "subsistence" dealers, "people who sell only small quantities, either to accommodate a friend (who may turn out to be a police agent) or on a rather infrequent basis to support their own habits." Other "big-time dealers" included are the "ambitious greenhorns, namely some college youth who buys a supply of heroin with dreams of setting himself up as a campus distributor. The amateur heroin dealer is a criminal but hardly a master or important criminal. He does stupid things; he has little background in crime; he might not even know how to deal with the realities of an arrest or an interrogation. He is a lone and ineffective operator. These 'accommodation,' 'subsistence' and 'amateur' dealers perform one important function. They supply law officials with closed cases, results. If it weren't for them, police efforts against narcotics offenses would look even less productive than what they do."

Even the police methodology for handling narcotics offenses insures a much greater emphasis on lower-echelon arrests. Brown points out that "America's police agencies were founded in a day when their task was seen as that of reacting to isolated events which disturbed the order of the community, and in a society simple enough so that this activity was adequate to maintain peace." The present situation is utterly different, but the police are paid to work in a way which is still largely a matter of individual battles against individual criminals over individual crimes. Detective A listens to a complaint, investigates, makes an arrest if circumstances warrant, and closes the case. Detective B "catches" and processes the next case. By this methodology, police departments and policemen individually see their work as the total of all the small tasks performed by the multitudes of "detectives A and B." Brown reports that narcotics sales are recorded as though they were all the same kind of operation. "The overall picture is given in terms of (1) *the number of crimes committed*; that is, narcotics sales reported (usually as compared to the number reported in the previous year); (2) *the number of arrests*; often given as a percentage of complaints, to achieve an index called the arrest rate, (the index is much better for narcotics sales than for most crimes, because few such sales are reported unless an arrest is made, whereas the police are notified of most burglaries or other serious victim crimes). Therefore, the police 'need' the continued illegalization of heroin, not only for the profit which it brings them, but also for the way in which their 'enforcement' record is 'improved.' And (3) *conviction rate*; that is, the percentage of convictions to arrests."

Instead of seeing all-important organizational and recurring patterned data, the viewer dealing with such statistical information sees thousands of isolated, indistinguishable incidents. Thus the criteria of good police performance become much clearer and easier to express than they should be. The police look "good" under "the following circumstances: if fewer crimes are reported—whether or not fewer crimes occur; if a greater number of arrests are made—whether or not the arrests are of important criminals; if there is a higher percentage of convictions—whether or not the convictions are for important crimes or of important criminals." The emphasis is on quantity, not quality.

Thus when the crimes or the criminals are organized into a system, police failure to make or deal with the connections of the system insures the continuation of the organization and its system since the organization is always much more important than any of the individual crimes it commits.

Police operations are seriously undermined by the "case-by-case approach. Even assuming no police corruption each investigator controls his own investigation, develops his own sources of information and quite frequently his own private files." As Brown says, "a narcotics unit working under such ground rules is not an organization directed to controlling narcotics sales. It is a grouping of individuals, each licensed to fish in the sea of narcotics crime. The other side of the coin is that the investigator is judged as an individual producer rather than as the member of a team." Combine that with the quanity-over-quality emphasis and it becomes obvious that the police investigator must be concerned more with his individual "batting average" than with the needs of the community. Brown emphasizes that, *"The pressure on the investigator is not to eradicate or reduce crime* [emphasis added] but to develop his relationship to it so that he can secure the number of arrests and convictions that will prove him to be a good performer."

An additional but "inevitable result of the quota system," as Curran shows, "has been corruption." "A member of the narcotics division testified that, because of the quota system and the need for arrests in quantity, 'padding' and 'flaking' were commonplace." "Padding" is adding to the weight of narcotics found in the possession of an arrested defendant in order to raise the quantity seized from misdemeanor to felony weight (over one-eighth of an ounce). "Police are able to 'pad' by holding back portions of narcotics seized from defendants previously arrested in other cases."

One of the more prominent cases of a detective withholding and possessing heroin removed from pushers in the process of their being arrested is that of Eddie (Popeye) Egan, who was recently dismissed from the Police Department following his role in the movie *The French Connection*. Egan had been charged with the possession of heroin, specifically, failure to turn in confiscated narcotics.

"Flaking" involves arresting an individual on the charge of possessing narcotics that were in fact placed on his person by the arresting officer. " 'Flaking' is, of course, a euphemism for framing and is a vicious product of the quota system. Flaking is rationalized on the grounds that the individual arrested is 'known' to be involved in narcotics traffic and it is therefore irrelevant as to whether he actually possesses narcotics when arrested."

Occasionally, however, people not at all involved in the drug business are threatened with a "flake." The Knapp Commission reported one officer approached a man selling wigs on the streets of Harlem and threatened him with a "flake" unless he provided narcotics tips.

There were more than the conventional forms of bribery noted. As a reverse form of flaking, one New York City policeman-chemist who worked in the police laboratory accepted a $120,000 bribe in exchange for falsifying the police lab report to indicate that the confiscated substance was not a narcotic when in fact it was.

An example of the division's ineffectiveness was found in the operations of its undercover unit, whose members buy heroin in the street and then arrest the seller. "In 1970 the New York City police made 7,266 separate purchases of heroin which resulted in 4,007 arrests. A grand total of 4.97 pounds of highly adulterated heroin (about eight ounces of pure heroin) was purchased in this fashion for $91,197.50 in cash—a cost of over $11,000 per ounce to say nothing of the staggering costs in terms of undercover surveillance officers, chemists, district attorneys and the courts. These purchases were made from addicts at the very lowest level of the narcotics traffic. The cases which resulted from these purchases clearly had no impact whatsoever on the heroin traffic in New York City . . . and thus the undercover operation has been demonstrably wasteful and wholly ineffective."

In spite of the failure of the undercover purchase program, on January 12, 1971, Commissioner Murphy announced that there would be "significant increases in the amount of money undercover policemen are permitted to use when purchasing heroin." Murphy was questioned whether this increase in the availability of money for heroin purchase or any other anticorruption method he introduced or planned to introduce would reduce the flow of heroin into the city. Murphy responded, "We're not sure, the supply coming in seems to be almost unlimited."

A possible negative feature of "undercover" purchases was pointed out by a Michigan county commissioner who suggested that police purchases for heroin generally inflated the price of drugs, "only driving up the price of the drugs, resulting in an increase in crime to pay for more expensive narcotics."

The State Commission said such undercover "buy and bust" operations of narcotics purchases "automatically eliminates the possibility of climbing up the ladder and reaching the upper echelons of drug criminals"—which is perhaps why such operations continue; they meet arrest quotas without touching big time criminals with "political connections."

An additional negative feature of undercover narcotics police work is seen in the case of Henry Marzette, a former Detroit cop who built a heroin empire with bribery, murder, and most importantly, policeman's undercover training. As long as heroin is illegal, undercover police work will be necessary for any attempt to control it, but at the same time its illegalization insures its profitability, which often proves to be more attractive to policemen than police work. In the case of Marzette, he started as a hero undercover narcotics cop setting departmental records for drug arrests and ultimately became king of Detroit's largest heroin distribution system, raking in $5 million a year. Marzette went from a $100-a-week cop, arresting both minor and major pushers, to the most important dealer in town. According to the *Detroit Free*

Press, "He was feared on the street as a man who lived arrogantly above the law." His success was built on his undercover police work. "He had the right kind of information about certain people in certain places to do it . . . A lot of people will breathe a lot easier now that Marzette kicked off. [He had just died in April 1972 of natural causes.] He could have blown the lid right off this town. He was never convicted of any serious crime. Marzette engineered his business in such a way that he minimized his risk. He knew about set-ups from having worked as an undercover cop, so he never told anyone in advance when he was delivering his heroin. He just showed up with it and collected later. And he always collected."

Because of the negative effects of police undercover narcotics work, the French, according to Congressman Robert Steele, do not allow "even police *officials* to become directly involved in investigation of narcotics traffic. If they do, they are liable to criminal prosecution. In the opinion of French governmental officials, the nature of the problem is such that the less known about police methods and tactics, the better the chances are for successful results. As a result, French police throughout the country sometimes work on narcotics cases without being completely aware of all the facts surrounding the case. This helps to prevent police corruption."

An example of upper-echelon police deficiency and/or corruption was seen in the State Commission's "discoveries of very substantial discrepancies between amounts of narcotics reported seized by arresting officers and the amounts subsequently reported by the police department laboratory. In a Commission survey of one unit of the narcotics division for 1970, out of eight selected cases, the Commission discovered a discrepancy of sixty-eight pounds of heroin between the arresting officers' reports and the amounts subsequently found by the police department chemists." The sixty-eight pounds assumes considerable proportions when one recalls that the entire undercover unit managed to purchase only 4.97 pounds of adulterated heroin in a one year's period.

Curran acknowledged that direct and overt corruption was a problem for the narcotics division at all levels. Assistant Chief Inspector Joseph McGovern and Chief of Patrol Donald Cawley said that "the biggest single problem of the narcotics division is corruption" and that "police corruption in narcotics cases had outpaced police corruption in gambling cases."

The situation looks somewhat gloomier when one suspects that in fact narcotics and gambling corruption often may involve the same upper-echelon police personnel. For example, former New York City Assistant Chief Inspector Thomas C. Renaghan faces a one-year prison term stemming from an investigation into police corruption *and* gambling. Up until his recent retirement, Renaghan had headed the narcotics division. He was, according to the *New York Post*, "appointed to the narcotics job from an anti-gambling position in a departmental shakeup to correct irregularities in the division."

As an example of police corruption in narcotics, William P. Brown, a retired inspector of the New York City Police and now on the Criminal Justice faculty of the State University of New York at Albany, presented the following evidence in his article, "The Golden Arm of the Law":

"Diane was an attractive young divorcée with two children, a fiancé and a drug addiction problem. John, her fiancé, talked the matter over with Diane's parents and they agreed that only drastic steps could help. John went to the police narcotics division office, reported Diane to Patrolman X and helped X arrest her. It was a bitter course of action, but John reasoned that it would mean for her compulsory treatment and a new life.

"The new life came, all right, but its main feature was Patrolman X. He saw Diane every day or so, having listed her officially as an informer so that their continuing association would not be questioned. It soon became apparent that he was supplying her with narcotics. When John complained to Patrolman X, he was beaten up and threatened with having his head blown off. Soon thereafter, another Patrolman, Y, began to come around, also supplying Diane with narcotics and enjoying her company. A short time later, X introduced Diane to Solly, a narcotics wholesaler for organized crime. They told her that they had 100 bags of heroin which she was to sell. When she protested, she was told to cooperate or they would 'take care of her.'

"The proceeds from the sale were split three ways among Diane, Patrolman X and Solly who—it later turned out— was another narcotics officer. When an official complaint was made, the plot turned even thicker. The policeman partners in crime kidnapped Diane and held her in an apartment for several days in an attempt to stop the investigation."

As former heroin addict and author William S. Burroughs notes on all the above corruption situations: "The narcs need the syndicate and the syndicate needs the narcs to keep the tired, expensive show on the road."

In addition to the above and to "flaking" and "padding," the State Commission disclosed the following forms of police corruption:

"Accepting bribes from narcotics defendants or prospective defendants."

"Extorting money and narcotics from narcotics violators in exchange for not making arrests and then reselling the narcotics." One witness at the Knapp Commission hear-

ings noted that when officers arrested a dealer and extorted his money and narcotics, it was considered good
form to leave the dealer "happy, by leaving him some of
his heroin so he could get back into business."

"Supplying heroin to others for use or re-sale, often in
exchange for stolen property such as televisions, cameras,
or cases of liquor." In an almost humorous situation one
cop ordered from his dealer-informant partner, in exchange for some heroin, two shipments of liquor to be sent
to his home. Unfortunately, the cop was not able to receive one of the shipments because he had to attend an
anticorruption meeting at the station house.

Addict informants were often used as officers' heroin
salesmen. Addict informants, according to the Knapp
Commission, are addicts who steal to order for policemen.
The police pay them off with heroin the police have seized
from other addicts and pushers. Theoretically a narcotics
informant is recruited by an individual policeman, who
registers the man in his station house by name and number. Thereafter, the theory goes, the policeman pays the
informant from a forty-dollar-a-month expense account.

The informant is supposed to work for no one else. But
according to Knapp Commission testimony, addicts wan-
dered between several station houses, making deliveries
and proposing impromptu dope-for-goods transactions
when an expected customer did not show.

A captain in the narcotics division told the Commission
that the number of informants employed was "almost a
military secret." But since an informant is "absolutely necessary" to make an airtight narcotics arrest, many officers
maintain more than one of them.

One dismissed patrolman who was a witness before the
Knapp Commission said he could not "begin to count" the
addict informers he knew in Harlem. "Sometimes I came

to the station house before 5 o'clock and the addict-in-formers would be standing around, asking me, 'Let's go on that operation, let's go on that operation,' because they wanted a fix. They worked for a fix . . . so they would come begging you to go on an operation with them," he said.

Former Inspector William Brown says that most informants are small-time drug dealers who are arrested and then agree to inform in exchange for leniency and money. Brown adds that "if the policeman is to get information of value, and even if he follows the most stringent professional guidelines that have been proposed, he must pay the informant well and he knows that the payment money will go into narcotics. *In theory*, the police officer pays for the information and the informant knows that he will be arrested if the officer gets wind of any further narcotics violation on the informant's part. *In practice* such a position is so unrealistic that it borders on the ridiculous."

Brown asks us to consider the following factors:

Since the police department will authorize only very small amounts of pay-off money to informants, "the most acceptable medium of payment is drugs." This seems to be particularly true when a big case is about to come off. Brown says "it is difficult to conceive of a situation wherein a sophisticated informant knew that a substantial seizure of drugs was likely to result from his information, and as long as he had a few hours to make the contacts, did not arrange to receive a portion of contraband as his payment."

Once an officer starts paying informants in narcotics, he must get them from somewhere. The State Commission elicited from several officers the statement that "an officer needing narcotics could ordinarily get them from another member of the squad." For continuing needs, however, only two sources are available: "The officer may confiscate drugs from a dealer and/or he can hold out on evidence.

Obviously, the drugs supplied as a favor by other officers must have come from similar sources. With the officers' power over an addict-informant, the addicts desperate and single minded attention to his own need and the standard practice which places the policeman who has a narcotics assignment in a continuing illegal relationship with a series of seller informants, the overall risk for the honest policeman is like that of living in a leper colony—infection may not occur but the possibility is extremely high."

As Suzannah Lessard in *Washington Monthly* points out, the odds for police corruption are very high. "In the course of duty a police agent is bound to come across stashes worth 50 times their weight in gold, not to mention large sums of money. On the other hand, an addict is easily manipulated by the police. By promising him his fix one can get him to betray his closest associates, a nasty practice which only escalates the mistrust and violence of the subculture and never leads to the upper echelon of a drug ring which, for this very reason, is scrupulously non-addict. Yet none of this is necessarily peculiar to heroin. If there were 600,000 diabetics in the country and insulin were declared illegal, the same situation would quickly develop."

While Brown makes clear how individual officers are corrupted, he does not, however, deal with the methods by which an entire police and prosecution system becomes corrupted, or the reasons therefor. More on this later. Other forms of police corruption found by the Curran Commission are:

"Directly selling heroin."

"Purchasing heroin from organized crime figures."

"Retaining heroin or money or both seized during a raid or search."

"Providing protection to those engaged in heroin transaction, for payment either in money or stolen property."

"Tipping of heroin violators of impending police raids and supplying other confidential police information to heroin violators, again in exchange for money, heroin, or stolen property."

"Interceding with brother police officers on behalf of narcotics criminals."

"Attempting to bribe assistant district attorneys and other public officials in narcotics cases."

"Sending narcotics to another state for sale."

"Committing perjury by giving false testimony in court in order to have a narcotics defendant acquitted, and presenting weak affidavits or compaints in order to bring about a lessening or dimissal of charges."

"Falsely alleging undercover purchases of narcotics in order to retain some of the purchase money supplied by the police department."

In addition to the above, Associated Press newsman Carl Zeitz reports "prison narcotics pushers get their heroin supply from state corrections officers. It's ten dollars and five cartons of cigarettes for a bag of heroin."

As Curran points out, the police and prosecution spare no effort to protect their fellow officers at all levels. For example: "In one case a detective who was a member of the police department for some fifteen years was indicted for the felony of conspiring to sell heroin. After resigning from the force he was permitted to plead guilty to the misdemeanor charge of official misconduct, was promptly sentenced to an unconditional discharge, and walked out of the courtroom a free man." Curran says this man was "cashiered to freedom."

At the hearing of this officer, "other witnesses and the convicted police officer himself testified that he had been selling heroin for at least a year prior to his arrest, having gone into partnership with two other police officers. The detective admitted quite readily that this was a business arrangement" involving both the purchasing and selling of heroin, to and from organized crime. "This one detective alone sold more heroin in 1970 than the entire narcotics division's undercover unit removed through their purchases from street vendors in the city in the same period of time." And as the Knapp Commission has reported, the majority of officers in the narcotics division were involved in one way or another in illegal heroin traffic, thereby making law enforcement, whether by purchase of heroin and/or arrests, irrelevant and impossible.

In the face of threats of public exposure of massive police corruption, the Knapp Commission was appointed by Mayor Lindsay a few days prior to the beginning of a *New York Times* series on police corruption based on information from New York City Detective David Durk. Durk said, "We came to *The Times* after every other city agency that was supposed to do something about police corruption failed to respond."

Both Knapp and Curran reported that it was "customary for police officers making narcotics arrests to be offered bribes." In spite of this fact, and in spite of the fact that there were well over fifty thousand narcotics arrests made between 1967 and 1969, only two arrests had been made for bribery attempts of police officers during that time span. However, in 1970, when there were in that year alone over seventy thousand narcotics arrests, there were only eight arrests made for attempted bribery of police officers. However, seven of the eight arrests occurred *after* revelations of police corruption had been reported by David Burnham of *The New York Times.*

The Curran Commission, in summary, notes:

"As a result of our extensive and public hearing the Commission concluded that the narcotics division had failed to do its job. We found this to be the case, *even without regard to the problem of corruption* [emphasis added]. With the corruption factor added the situation has become a disaster."

The Knapp Commission's findings not only paralleled Curran's conclusions but in fact expanded upon them. For example:

1. A New York City police captain testified that there is a pattern of organized corruption within the city's narcotics units and the Federal Government's.

2. The elite twenty-man Preventative Enforcement Patrol (PEP), formed to fight narcotics pushing, ". . . was almost totally corrupted, with eighteen of the twenty patrolmen taking bribes ranging from $1,500 to $3,000 a month, and the remaining two officers sharing in the illegal profits."

3. Detective David Durk reported that some illegal heroin operators had given policemen "many thousands of dollars" to learn how much the special investigating units knew about their operations. The heroin dealers sought the information so they could change their procedures before any raid. Durk reported this information to his superiors. Not only was no action taken, but also, Durk noted, "I understand the case was closed." A police captain, however, threatened "to break my back if I ever embarrassed his command."

4. In terms of narcotics law enforcement the Knapp Commission noted that in all squads and patrols relating to narcotics laws is ". . . a picture of corruption so systematized it has become for many officers almost a way of life, a thing so accepted it seemed to many officers almost senseless to resist the taking of benefits."

The New York Times editorialized that "in many precincts it was easier to be corrupt than to be honest. What is tragically clear is that the pattern of corruption is so ingrained in some police operations that those officers who refuse to share in illegal payments are in danger of becoming pariahs in their units."

In an earlier attempt to understand police corruption, Yale sociologist Dr. Albert J. Reiss, who has been studying police matters for more than ten years, trained thirty-six observers and sent them into three large American cities to record systematically everything that occurred when policemen and citizens met. When the study was nearly completed, Dr. Reiss told some members of the President's Crime Commission that significant numbers of policemen had been seen committing serious crimes and violating departmental rules, despite the policemen's knowledge that they were *under direct observation* by staff people from the President's Crime Commission. A few staff members joked that committing these crimes in the presence of the observers was final proof of the stupidity of the police. But, as David Burnham, police reporter for *The New York Times* noted, "Reiss dismissed this condescension. He proposed the far more chilling theory that the calm acceptance of the observers showed that misconduct was so regular and routine that the police failed to understand that it was improper. Reiss' findings suggest the vast difference between the reality of police work and the public picture of it painted by hypocritical politicians and self-serving police officials."

So pervasive was the level of narcotics corruption found in New York City that First Deputy Police Commissioner William H.T. Smith declared that ". . . the department definitely rejected the 'rotten apple' theory." As a result of the publicity and public outrage produced by the Knapp

Commission hearings, a few honest officers in the Police Department said that, "Not very long ago we talked about corruption with all the enthusiasm of a group of little old ladies talking about venereal disease. Now there is a lot more open discussion about combating corruption as if it were a public health problem."

5. While the Knapp Commission was instructed to look into all aspects of police corruption, the largest single category of complaints was for narcotics payoffs.

6. Captain Daniel McGowen testified that under former Police Commissioner Howard R. Leary there had been a steady *decrease* in the number of anticorruption investigators in the Police Department. McGowen theorized that the decrease stemmed from "internal political pressure" by law enforcement unions, such as the Patrolmen's Benevolent Association and the Sergeants' Benevolent Association.

7. McGowen testified that some officers who have come forward to inform their superiors about corruption going on within their units find that the superior will send the honest cop to a police psychiatrist in an attempt to discourage any further interest in corruption.

8. A New York City police inspector, C.J. Behan, testified before the Knapp Commission that he had passed on reports of widespread narcotics and gambling corruption to the second highest official in the Police Department, John F. Walsh, who produced no overt or covert response for over eight months. After eight months with still no response from Walsh, an investigation was begun by Behan and Detective Frank Serpico. Walsh's response to Behan's report, he told the Knapp Commission, was: "It left my mind." However, Walsh said that the "existence of an honest policeman who was willing to investigate corruption, especially in his own unit, was highly unusual.

I don't recall any other similar case of a policeman who actually came forward unsolicited and wanted to do something about police corruption. What Serpico was doing was unique in the Department's history," Walsh said, in spite of the Department's decades' long history of police corruption as documented in the City's newspapers.

Walsh admitted that he never met Serpico until long after the Knapp Commission was in progress, even though Walsh knew that Serpico was gathering information that ". . . showed that not a squad, nor even a precinct, *but an entire police division of plainclothesmen was corrupt* [emphasis added]. Congressman Charles W. Rangel of Harlem said police corruption was so massive that people in his community "could not go to a single police officer to turn in a pusher and believe that the pusher would be arrested."

9. Detective Frank Serpico gave similar detailed information of police narcotics corruption to Jay Kriegel, a close associate of, and advisor to, Mayor John Lindsay, and to Arnold G. Fraiman, then City investigation commissioner and now a State Supreme Court Justice. "In neither case was there any apparent result," the detective testified, even though first-hand evidence of involvement of police lieutenants and captains was presented. Serpico said that Captain Phillip Foran, assigned to the Department of Investigation, had threatened Serpico that he (Serpico) would end up "face down in the river" if he insisted upon testifying about police corruption. Walsh also refused to investigate this allegation or tell any other high officials about it. Knapp Commission investigators called Serpico a "live grenade" to top police officials.

10. According to a *New York Times* report of December 21, 1971, Detective Serpico, along with Detective David Durk, felt the necessity for the Knapp Commission inves-

tigations ". . . because they did not find a sympathetic ear among all the mayoral aides and high ranking police officials they had gone to in their effort to fight corruption in the Police Department."

New York City Councilman Matthew Troy, in the face of all this official inaction, demanded that District Attorney Frank S. Hogan study the Knapp Commission transcripts to determine whether high Lindsay administration officials were guilty of "perjury (misfeasance) and/or malfeasance." Hogan replied that all the transcripts were being studied for any violations of law. Troy also demanded "that Mayor Lindsay be forced to answer under oath why he failed to report all allegations of serious police corruption to any competent authority."

Durk poignantly stated that "At the very beginning, the most important fact to understand is that I had and have no *special* knowledge of police corruption. We knew nothing that wasn't known to every man and officer. We knew nothing about the police traffic in narcotics that wasn't known by most officers. We knew these things because we were involved in law enforcement in New York City and anyone in the whole Police Department who said he did not know about widespread corruption had to be blind, either by choice or by incompetence.

"We simply cannot believe, and we do not believe today, that those with authority and responsibility in the area, whether the District Attorneys, the police commanders, or those in power in City Hall, couldn't also have exposed these facts of corruption in six months, or at least in six years, that is, if they wanted to do it. The fact is that almost wherever we turned in the Police Department, wherever we turned in the city administration, we were met not with cooperation, not with appreciation, but with suspicion and hostility.

"We wanted to believe in a system of responsibility. But those in high places everywhere in the Police Department, in the District Attorney's office, in City Hall, were determined not to enforce the law. The system that was supposed to be protecting people was selling poison to their children. The system ruined men and made the department a home for drug dealers.

"Of course, all corruption is bad, but we cannot fall into the trap of pretending that all corruption is equally bad. There is a difference between bribing with free meals and bribing with narcotics. If we are unable to make that distinction then we are saying to the police that the life of a child in the South Bronx has the same moral value as a cup of coffee.

"Tow-truck operators can write off bribes to cops on their income tax. The expense-account executive can afford a prostitute. But nobody can repay a mother for the pain of seeing her children hooked on heroin."

Durk pleaded with the Knapp Commission to fix "responsibility inside and outside the Police Department, *all the way up and down the chain of police, political and judicial command.*"

Durk recalled that, "Once I arrested a landlord who offered me a bribe if I would not arrest a tenant who was molesting a number of other tenants in the building. I put the cuffs on the landlord. A crowd of people were around, and actually said, '*Viva policia.*' Of course, it was not just me or even the police that they were cheering. They were cheering because they had glimpsed in that one arrest the *possibility* of a system of justice that could work to protect them."

Of course police addiction corruption is not confined to New York City. For example, the *Albany Knickerbocker News-Union Star* recently launched a two-week series on the relationship in the state's capital between heroin and police corruption.

The first story began: ". . . local drug enforcement here is a monumental flop—heroin availability and use are soaring; major pushers remain free to brazenly peddle their wares; heroin-related crime and associated serious police corruption are spreading out of control." Policemen in Albany were quoted as saying what policemen in New York City were admitting before cameras: It's easier for a cop to become crooked than to remain honest—particularly when narcotics are involved.

According to an investigative reporter for the Albany paper, K. Scott Christianson:

"Narcotics corruption is the newest and most lucrative variant of an age-old affliction; most observers consider it the worst." If New York City and Albany are any indication, every city and suburb would do well to examine its own vulnerability to drugs and its related crime waves. For example, radio station WSB in Atlanta announced on November 10, 1971, that it would air a few nights later an hour-long news special: "Atlanta's Drug Problem—What Do We Do About It?" Atlanta, the press release stated, has become known as a major heroin distribution center for its region.

Even remote Anchorage, Alaska, can sustain a growing addict population of twenty-five hundred—including a nine-year-old boy.

As Christianson points out, "Albany has a population of 100,000 and a police department of 240 men." With expanding ghettoization, Albany is now without one movie theater and is clearly limited in its social, recreational, welfare, and medical resources. Narcotics problems have consequently skyrocketed. Concomitantly, Albany's venereal disease rates now surpass those of New York City.

A major reason, of course, for the rapid rise in VD is a sharp escalation in prostitution—one of the city's few older trades that have grown, not died. There are more prostitutes now because more and more women must sell their bodies to buy dope.

Professor William P. Brown at the local State University agrees with other criminologists who say that recent police corruption disclosures, particularly when related to narcotics, are symptomatic of serious breakdowns throughout the law enforcement system.

Christianson says, "When mixed with crooked police, heroin induces a cynicism that fosters contempt for all law enforcement—and a bonanza for organized criminals. Heroin and police corruption are both toxic in themselves and when combined can be lethal."

Dr. Francis A.J. Ianni, professor of education at Columbia University, has noted in surveys of Harlem school children that most slum kids attribute the narcotics problem to a genocidal conspiracy against the blacks, initiated by the white power structure and carried off with the aid of the police. Militant Albany blacks imply the same. The blacks ask: "Why is it? A two bit junkie from Memphis, Tennessee, or Kalamazoo, Michigan, comes here and buys heroin in half an hour. But the cops can't get to the same pusher, even though he's been the biggest dealer here for years."

The Albany newspaper broke the local story with the aid of a few former policemen, publishing a series of ten articles about police corruption, prostitution, and other drug-related crimes.

Christianson noted that reaction to the series, which ended ten days before election day, was intense. Mayor Corning attacked the disclosures as "trash," "yellow journalism," and "horror science fiction." The newspaper received a heavy response from the police. Cops referred to as crooked in the series passed threats back through middlemen.

Some of the more alarming disclosures came from a former city narcotics squad informant—alarming because of the iceberg tip it represented. For security reasons, the informant was identified only as a person whose information had resulted in numerous felony convictions for Albany detectives, and whose reliability had been upheld by a judge as sufficient to justify the issuance of search warrants. As reported by Christianson, the informant said:

"Detective J., Albany narco squad, told me he wanted all my information in writing, so I typed it up for him. It had everything in there. Next thing I know one of the area's biggest pushers comes up to me on the street with this stack of papers. 'You recognize these?' he says. I said, 'What are you talkin' about, man—I never seen them.' But it scared holy hell out of me, 'cause them was the same papers I gave Detective J. You could tell by the lousy typewriting and it was the same exact paper. I just told him I didn't know what he was talking about and walked away like I didn't care. But then Mister Big put the word out he wants to see me. That it's real important . . ."

Three other informants charged that city detectives had intentionally blown the informants' covers, or set them up to be killed by pushers. They also noted cases in which crooked detectives had tipped off pushers and pimps about scheduled raids.

Extensive interviews with Albany policemen and prostitutes alike revealed that many city detectives for decades have collected large sums from brothels and prostitutes for "protection." Also 50 percent of the city's prostitutes are known to be addicts forced to do robberies and other crimes to help support their habits. Also shown was that the biggest heroin dealers were known to be the biggest pimps; they often used prostitutes to traffic in dope for them. Asked why the biggest pushers had been so successful at avoiding arrest, one patrolman replied that one of the main reasons was that "The pushers have the girls (prostitutes) and the girls are paying the cops. If the cops bust the pushers, the cops take money out of their own pockets."

Christianson points out that there are additional reasons why the narcotics business is such a relatively safe one: "In Albany, as in most cities with a major narcotic problem, heroin is found principally in the black slum." Since racism is as American as cherry pie and violence, it is not surprising that there are no black policemen on Albany's narcotics squad. Thus infiltration into the black community by a white cop would be both difficult and dangerous. "Top dealers are cautious: they often use junkies and prostitutes to act as their covers; they seldom sell to strangers—especially white ones."

Some pushers carry large sums of "fall money," designed to bribe policemen, if caught. Some become informants, in order to help the police make the necessary number of arrests (quota system), while themselves keeping clear of trouble. Albany's top pusher and pimp, a four-time offender, managed to escape a possible life prison term by wrongfully claiming to be an addict, and thus having himself sent to a state rehabilitation clinic.

The dilemma of many Albany cops extends beyond the laws and procedures that have put all policemen at a marked disadvantage. "The men are afraid to talk," one veteran said. "It's because the system plays so dirty—they let the men become corrupt and actually want them to, so they can keep them under their thumb. The men are scared to move as a result—they've got too much to hide."

Others complained of codes of silence that contributed to making corruption inevitable.

Of course, police addiction corruption is not confined to New York City or New York State.

According to David Burnham of *The New York Times*: "Police corruption involving the selling of heroin has been uncovered recently in police departments and sheriff's offices in at least 23 states and the District of Columbia. But Dr. Albert J. Reiss . . . says the number of *official* investigations seriously understates the extent of police corruption." Reiss said that "It is my conviction that there is extensive corruption in almost every major and many medium-sized police departments in the United States. I am convinced that official investigations are a poor index of the size of the corruption problem."

Burnham points out that "because no single organization collects information about police corruption investigations going on throughout the country, many of them may not be noted. Even the Justice Department reports, for example, that it does not know how many policemen have been indicted in the last year by *Federal* prosecutors or how many police corruption cases have been investigated by the F.B.I."

"The most recent Federal investigation of police corruption to become known is in Chicago, where nine policemen were suspended three weeks ago (early January 1972) after refusing to answer the questions of a Federal grand jury that is investigating police involvement in the sale of narcotics. At the same time that the nine were suspended, Chicago Police Superintendent James Conlisk demoted two high police officials to their civil service rank of captain, including the *commander of the Department's anti-corruption unit* [emphasis added].

"In Los Angeles, Federal agents arrested a police intelligence officer on charges of possessing pure heroin with a retail value of $320,000."

In Detroit, according to Jeff Kamen of the Public Information Center: "Police officers are making enormous profits from the sale of heroin in the Motor City's ghetto. A grand jury investigation of police corruption has been underway for some time, but indications are that the probe will barely touch the surface of the deeply rooted involvement of many Detroit policemen of virtually every rank. The investigation has been conducted by the Wayne County prosecutor and he, after all, is part of an administration that to date has passed the buck or dismissed the allegations as trivial.

"One 18-year-old pusher told me, 'the vice squad knocked on the door and I had to let them in. I had a houseful of people and they were shootin' up, snorten'. The police took me into the back room and said if I didn't pay them off they would bust me.'

"Another dealer told me this story: 'The police kicked my door down and a lot of people were sitting around shootin' up and I was too. So they asked who was the owner of the house. To keep everyone else out of trouble, I spoke up and said I was the owner. They called me into a room and asked me how much business I was doing. I told them I was only doing a small business, enough to support my own habit and the habits of my two girls. The head cop informed me that if I didn't pay him $200 a week my place would be busted down. So they left and they didn't take anybody down. There were works [the tools of addiction such as hypo, spoon, etc.] all over the place, dope all over the place. They just left. I didn't pay any attention to their telling me to pay them off. So, a couple of weeks later, they came again. This time they totally wrecked my house and said if I didn't pay them

$200 a week they would put me in jail and everyone in the house in jail also. So I got kinda shakey in that place and I moved out of that place into another one. And they found me there.'

"Dr. Wayne Hollinger is a private physician running a methadone clinic for 750 addicts keeping 750 junkies off heroin. Thus it is under heavy attack from the police. Hollinger's patients have been stopped by police officers, searched, their methadone taken from them and either stolen outright or scattered on the sidewalk and crushed under heel.

"One of Hollinger's patients reported that she had been visited by three plainclothes policemen who forced their way into her apartment and asked her to go out and sell the methadone tablets she was given by Dr. Hollinger. 'They told me,' she said, 'they had to get Dr. Hollinger, because he was screwing everything up.' Selling methadone by a non-physician is as illegal as pushing heroin. They could have arrested her for it and ruined Hollinger's reputation and program at the same time. When she refused, two of the officers left, but the third man remained to try a different tact. 'He told me if I didn't go along with them and if I didn't go to bed with him he'd bust me.'

"Hollinger said, 'I must be hurting the dope dealers more than I figured. When you estimate the average junkie in this area spends $50 a day for stuff and multiply that by 750 addicts, you get a big chunk of cash the hoodlums aren't getting any more.' Using Hollinger's figures, the yearly take from 750 junkies is $13,687,500.

"A pusher who eventually quit pushing told me his life as a dealer was 'alright as long as you paid the police off. They would come to my place like once a week to get paid off and as long as I paid, everything was cool. I paid them $300 a week every week for two years.' [Using his figures,

that four-man team of plainclothesmen extorted $31,000
from his dope house alone and undoubtedly had several
more on their 'protection' list.]

"The ex-pusher went on: 'like I was doing pretty good.
I paid them $300 weekly and made about $400 for myself.
So I really didn't miss it. It really was kinda smooth, you
know?' He was never charged with selling or using drugs.

"An old precinct house joke goes like this, 'You'd better
not arrest no pushers, rookie, or the captain's gonna have
your ass.' Congressmen Claude Pepper said about police
addiction corruption: 'I think I can guarantee that it goes
at least up to the precinct commander, to the captain level.'
A former pusher was asked, 'Could you have operated
without police help?' The ex-dealer responded, 'Man, are
you serious?' "

The real price of police corruption, says Detective Durk,
is "not free meals or broken regulations but dying neighborhoods and a whole generation of children being lost."

Adam Walinsky, aide to the late Senator Robert F.
Kennedy, says of police corruption:

"After years of pretending that the heroin traffic was
an unavoidable if tragic blight, a kind of Harlem Dutch-
elm disease, we have been forced to face the truth. The
narcotics that kill thousands of New York's children, that
makes much of the city a hell-on-earth where junkies steal
and mug for the price of a fix—the traffic in these drugs is
protected by police, is participated in by police, and has
become the largest source of illicit police income. Obviously high police commanders have been either involved
or incompetent. The whole department is rotten.

"But these shocking facts are also old facts; *only their
public exposure is new. Ten years ago* [emphasis added]
Dick Gregory asked, 'If every nine-year-old in Harlem
knows who's selling dope, why don't the cops know?' The

plain answer, that they knew all too well, could have been given by many—knowledgeable law enforcement officials, politicians, reporters, and lawyers. For example, as New York's *Village Voice* editorialized: 'There can be no excusing New York City Council President Sandford Garelik, a former Chief Inspector of Police, who must have known what was going on, but who voted against the Knapp inquiry.' The real question, therefore, is: If the people in so-called responsible positions knew it all along, and did nothing, then what are the real prospects for change today.

"The answer is, not good—for many of the same reasons that have kept the facts effectively secret for all these long years. For police corruption to have spread so far, a lot of deliberate blindness was essential. Mayor Lindsay and his administration had to decide to ignore it—the price, they thought, of police restraint in the long hot summers. In the reported words of one high official, 'Let the animals steal, so long as it's quiet in Brownsville.' Their racism, of course, couldn't have been more blatant.

"At the higher levels, narcotics is a matter of organized crime—not just the Mafia, but also Jews, Irishmen, wasps, blacks, Latins, with connections to respectable lawyers, judges, labor leaders, and businessmen. Even honest politicians tend to be uncomfortable with real investigations of organized crime; they could end up investigating too many of their friends, allies, and contributors. Better not to know.

"Second, politicians do not like to alienate large blocs of voters. The Policemen's Benevolent Association is a powerful political force. So politicians, especially those on the law-and-order right, are silent on police corruption, even when it kills children.

"Third, there is a lot of misplaced good manners and

general hypocritical high-mindedness. Even so-called non-political newspapers, lawyers, and government officials do not make blanket accusations (even when appropriate), do not impugn the reputation of an *entire police force* [emphasis added], or of the criminal bar, or of the courts, by suggesting that there is a disease running through them all.

"One of the fundamental reasons for official inaction against the drug traffic is that its victims are just not that important to much of the white public. Narcotics addiction has been with us for over twenty years, but it has spread widely beyond the ghettos only in the last two or three years. Up until very recently, the dead, the dying, and the diseased have been just *them*, blacks and Latins, someone else's kids.

"And there are other less dramatic victims: the police themselves. They have been killers, above all, of their own hopes, their own self-respect, their own dreams of pride and excellence. Ninety percent or more of them left the Police Academy with such dreams. But they were abandoned to the massive pressures of a corrupt system.

"The Knapp Commission must go beyond exposing police corruption to examine *why* it was allowed to flourish unexamined and unchecked. We must go to the top and beyond, not because the responsibility belongs to the Mayor, but because he shares it with so many others. He shares it with the silent politicians, and the more silent lawyers, and the newspapers who are willing to pillory patrolmen but not the real decision makers."

The importance of the Knapp Commission, as with the Pentagon Papers, lies not in its exposing new information. After all, any of New York City's four hundred thousand junkies, not to mention tens of thousands of community organizers, social workers, and ghetto residents knew on a day-to-day basis that cops and narcs were heavily involved in pushing and protecting heroin traffic. By the same token hundreds of thousands of radicals, reporters, and politicians knew the government was lying through its teeth about Vietnam, long before the Pentagon Papers were released.

What the Knapp Commission and the Pentagon Papers did expose was the lengths to which various and several administrations go to protect themselves from any blame coming their way, blame for the corruption they were legally responsible for and criminally negligent in not fully exposing. When an issue as important as the war in Vietnam or the addiction crisis at home is covered up and/or distorted by and/or is a result of major government officials and their policies, of both major parties, at all levels, then that system of government must be questioned.

The police, of course, are only one agency of all the law enforcement agencies allegedly designed to combat drug traffic. What about the offices of the prosecution, the district attorneys? As New York reporter Mary P. Nichols wrote: "One thing the Knapp Commission will not do is expose fixable or incompetent D.A.'s. The Knapp Commission is limited both by its original scope—to investigate charges made against the police force—and by money and time. Nevertheless, who will investigate why the amount of police corruption that was revealed in Manhattan during the Knapp hearings somehow escaped the vigilance of District Attorney Frank S. Hogan? And who will investigate Hogan's recent raid on the home of Knapp assistant Teddy Ratnoff, where Hogan's men removed the evidence that Ratnoff had on Hogan's friend Judge Mitchell Schweitzer?"

Prominent New York civil liberties attorney Martin Garbus developed the case against District Attorney

Hogan. Hogan's questionable behavior is important in terms of the international symbol of uncorruptibility that Hogan represented, and in view of the fact that what is occurring in New York City can in no way be considered unique.

Garbus in *New York* magazine complained that the Knapp Commission showed specifically only how widespread police corruption was (and is) and that the Commission shed no light on any reasons *why* "police corruption is so pervasive and so deeply entrenched." What concerns Garbus is the methods of "law enforcement that makes corrupt behavior by a policeman on the street not very different from his behavior in, say, a court of law," that is, that police perjury in court is routine. Garbus says: "I'm trying to say that if cops make deals to give perjured testimony in court I don't think we are entitled to be surprised that they deal in dope on the street." What the Knapp Commission could show us if it investigated District Attorney Hogan is "that the way justice is administered in New York—the system—makes it appallingly easy for a cop to be corrupt. And Hogan's office is a tremendous factor in that system, and yet Hogan will not be called before the Knapp Commission. I'm saying specifically because of Hogan's inattention and inaction he may have contributed greatly to the problem of cleaning up the police force. Hogan has been derelict in his duty. Hogan has been indifferent to or *deliberately unconcerned with—if not consciously acquiescing in* [emphasis added]—criminal behavior within police ranks."

In terms of evidence Garbus notes that Knapp, with a staff of 12 and a budget of half a million dollars, has already turned up evidence resulting in twenty-two indictments on police corruption. Hogan's office, with an annual budget of $4.3 million and 147 lawyers and a nearly equal number of other personnel, including 70 New York City detectives, has, in the past seven years, succeeded in getting only thirty-three indictments against corrupt policemen. And all this must be seen in the perspective of Hogan's creditable record in other areas of prosecution.

Garbus says that district attorneys in general, and Hogan in particular, feel differently about police criminality and civilian criminality. That's not such a surprising belief given the fact that D.A.s are elected often on their "performance record." If the D.A.s crack down on the cops, the cops might not make as many arrests as were politically needed, thereby placing the D.A.'s office in political jeopardy.

For example, as Garbus notes, the D.A.'s office will, as a matter of course, go out and make *independent* investigations of Black Panthers, but will not subpoena police precinct house records or even review court testimony looking for police wrongdoings.

In effect, nobody polices the police; the police are outside the law.

Such a double standard hardly encourages law-abiding policemen. As Garbus points out, respect for laws, not to mention justice, doesn't develop in a vacuum. "If the D.A. winks at police perjured testimony in a court of law to strengthen his case, respect for law or justice is thereby diminished. The cop who shades his testimony in the presence of the D.A.'s office and finds that nothing happens to him, may do a bit of shading on the street."

The most dramatic evidence supporting the notion that the D.A.'s office is aware of police perjury was seen in the way in which police testimony in narcotics cases changed after the Mapp decision a decade ago. Garbus says that "in 1961 the Supreme Court ruled that evidence obtained by the police through unreasonable searches and seizures could not be used in prosecution. Well, for a few months after that, New York policemen continued to tell the truth about the circumstances under which evidence came into their hands (i.e., through unreasonable searches)—with the result that a lot of evidence in a lot of cases was declared inadmissible in court."

Then the police made an important discovery. If a defendant dropped heroin on the ground, after which a policeman arrested him, then a search would be "reasonable" and any evidence seized admissible. Garbus says: "Spend a few hours in the New York Criminal Court nowadays and you will hear case after case in which a policeman, in response to a District Attorney's questions, testifies that the defendant-dropped-the-heroin-on-the-ground-whereupon-I-arrested-him. The very language of the testimony is very often identical from one case to another." This type of testimony has become so well known that it is labeled, by the defense and prosecution alike, "dropsy" testimony. Plainclothesmen reported a 72 percent increase in this type of testimony. "If a policeman can, with impunity, illegally search a suspect and turn over the evidence to the D.A., he can also take the evidence and—as the Knapp testimony has shown—turn it over to another pusher for resale and share in the proceeds."

According to Garbus the "dropsy" testimony isn't the only perjured testimony the police present in court. The number of "open door" testimonies now coming into criminal courts is astonishing. "If one were to believe all the cops who testify in narcotics cases, then nearly all the people living in ghetto apartments keep their doors open all the time. In case after case a cop will testify that when he entered the building and got to the defendant's floor and approached the apartment, he could see (from the doorway) narcotics on a table or on a sofa, because the door was open. This means the cop can go in and make the arrest. If the door were locked and if he didn't have a warrant, he could not enter the apartment. It just can't be that way in case after case, yet that kind of testimony goes on and on."

To make matters worse, even if the door were open there's no reason to believe the cop didn't simply "drop" the heroin once he got inside. The very area in which police perjury seems most common is precisely the area in which the Knapp Commisison found the most police corruption—narcotics. These sorts of perjury cases "happen so often that, at the very least the *pattern* of perjury must be known to the D.A. Unless there is a change in the D.A.'s attitude toward police perjury, changing the entire police force from top to bottom is not going to change greatly the problem of police narcotics corruption. When a policeman making an arrest can pick up $25,000 by shading his testimony in a narcotics case, the tendency will always be to shade the testimony. Or, after getting the narcotics, he can say the potential defendant got away. There must be institutional changes." Someone has to police the police *and* the prosecution. "We can have Knapp-type commissions and civilian review boards forever, but they won't change a thing."

Perhaps, not surprisingly, when Frank Hogan's office was prosecuting Lenny Bruce, Martin Garbus was the lawyer for Bruce who said: "In the halls of justice, the only justice is in the halls."

5 Junk and Genocide: Ghetto Counterinsurgency

In ghetto areas police and prosecution corruption is blatant, and thus narcotics law enforcement there is particularly ineffective. In a study of the Bedford-Stuyvesant ghetto area in Brooklyn, by Dr. Mary Maroni of the Policy Sciences Center, she found that 8 percent of the total annual income for all residents in Bedford-Stuyvesant goes for the purchase of heroin . . . an increase of 835 percent just since 1963.

In Harlem the situation is at least as bad. The New York Addicts Rehabilitation Center found that at least one in six people in Harlem was a heroin addict. As Harlem's Congressman Charles B. Rangel says: "Walk along any street uptown and you'll see Harlem's great addict army—slumped over in doorways, stumbling along in a trance, nodding in front of bars, standing in the cold without enough clothes on. Chances are you'll also see another all too familiar Harlem scene: the dope pusher who sets up shop on a street corner and deals like he has a license—and for all practical purposes he does, when one considers 'license fees' paid to the local police precinct; whole neighborhoods have been completely abandoned to junkies. Heroin has destroyed what little functioning our school system had. Eight-year-olds experiment with heroin bought in the grade school yard and in Benjamin Franklin High School, where dope is as available as chewing gum, young girls shoot up in the locker room and 13-year-olds buy dope from 15-year-old peddlers.

"According to a survey of Harlem conducted by the Small Business Chamber of Commerce, 51 percent of Harlem's residents have been mugged, where 70 percent of those assaults were by *known* addicts. Ninety percent of all businesses in central Harlem have been robbed or pilfered—again primarily by addicts.

"Despite the impression given by some popular newspaper and magazine articles, it is not the middle-class white who suffers most from addict rip-offs; it is the blacks and Puerto Ricans in the ghetto areas, where most of the addicts live.

"But most devastating of all is the effect heroin has had on our young—the hope of the black nation. It used to be that a mother would pray that her son would finish high school. Now, she dare not admit to herself, her worst fears: that her son's corpse will be found on some rooftop, a needle sticking from his arm. I personally know of a mother who has four sons, all of them addicts, and such a situation is not unique.

"The sad fact is that heroin is so readily available in Harlem that any kid with some curiosity is bound to try it. Dr. Paul A. Searcy testified before the National Commission on Drug Abuse that in Harlem heroin was easier to get than bread or milk. This should not be surprising given the fact that only modest profits can be made from nutritious foods, compared to the windfall that can be had with heroin.

"Despite much heralded pledges of intergovernmental cooperation to halt the international drug traffic, not a single heroin laboratory in France has been busted in the last 2–3 years [1971] and the amount of heroin smuggled into the United States from Southeast Asia is up sharply.

"The people of Harlem may or may not know of these intergovernmental non-functionings, but they do see the cops of Harlem, cops who are quite willing to defend the Republic against permissiveness and long hair, but who look the other way when a heroin sale is transacted. Cops who proudly wear the American flag, but accept payoffs or make a heroin bust and then resell what they've confiscated. That's the way it is in Harlem. The situation only gets worse and more and more of the young are shouting, 'genocide.' "

Why the word "genocide"? The dictionary definition of "genocide" is the *planned* extermination of a racial group. In the case of heroin, if physical extermination is not the goal, political, social, and cultural extermination seem to be the approaching result.

Presidential crime commissioner Dr. William R. Corson believes that we have vastly underestimated the number of addicts, that in fact there may be up to three million heroin addicts of whom at least 80 percent are black or members of a racial minority, and that it is the *youth* of these racial minorities who are most affected and afflicted. And of course it is the youth who are the most likely to develop a political consciousness to challenge the corporate status quo of America.

Corson says that "treatment can never wipe out the heroin traffic, that none of the treatment programs effect a net reduction in the number of addicts and that indeed treatment may contribute to an increase in addiction. For example, methadone treatment programs are distracting public attention from solutions to the drug problem. And worse, methadone hooks even harder than heroin. There have been virtually no successful withdrawals from methadone after substituting it for heroin. And if for any reason the methadone addict is unable to stay on methadone, he is likely to return to heroin in a bigger way than before."

Corson continues: Methadone has gained acceptance among many physicians and politicians because the methadone habit is legal and cheap compared to the illegal and expensive heroin habit. "However, when a heroin addict switches to methadone, the heroin pusher and distributing organization have lost a customer—a customer who needs and buys heroin seven days a week. These pushers and distributors aren't going to take a cut in their business. Every lost customer is going to be replaced. But with whom? Drug peddlers have made their market analysis and know where the sales resistance is low. So for several years they have been selling to younger and younger customers." This must be seen in the context of there being virtually no narcotics treatment facilities for youths under eighteen years old, while at the same time the average age of the addict drops each year.

Corson points out that what methadone advocates don't talk about is that vast, illegal diversions of methadone, though originally intended for oral consumption, are being intravenously injected with approximately the same addictive euphoria as heroin. Except that, because methadone is usually cheaper than heroin, the addict community is now becoming addicted to and dependent on *both* methadone *and* heroin. With the government at numerous levels controlling the distribution and diversion of both methadone and heroin, the opportunity for governmental pacification and counterinsurgency is greatly enhanced.

Corson notes that *profits* from the illegal sale of heroin

are "variously estimated at between 20 and 40 billion dollars annually. There is a view in some segments of government that the heroin interests are so powerful that they should not be challenged." In fact, one might say, "if you can't lick 'em, join 'em," which to a large degree is quite possibly what the government has done.

Historically, heroin has, at least apparently, played a unique role in the black struggle for liberation. There is some historical and current evidence to suggest that while the black communities have been struggling for community control, the government has been doing all in its power to maintain its corporate control over those communities.

Black communities have been becoming increasingly rebellious since the Civil Rights movement in 1959 in general, and in particular with the burning of Watts in 1965. According to author and social scientist Michael Rossman: "By 1968 there were riots in 120 cities when Martin Luther King was assassinated. Then the trend of burning and rioting seemed to be reversed. But the reversal of this trend must have required more than multiplied military force and managed news to pacify the ghettoes." It is Rossman's belief that "the relative peace since then has been enforced by massive injections of heroin into the black mainline. Before each 'long, hot summer' and in each period of ghetto political tension, heroin becomes increasingly available to the ghettoes. Addicts nod in doorways, people strengthen their locks in fear. Over 70 percent of all ghetto crime is heroin connected. The effect of all this injection of heroin is that the ghetto people's energies become absorbed *internally*, turned against itself, undermining all revolt against the external colonizing forces and the social conditions they have created."

Rossman continues: "The practice of drugging black

ghettoes with heroin seems to have begun seriously around 1967. The American Psychiatric Association reports that 'the extent of heroin use has grown wildly since the mid-1960's.' A long-time informer for the Los Angeles Police Department, whom the police publicly acknowledge as an informer, told *The New York Times* on October 24, 1971 that 'the police had allowed and encouraged narcotics to be sold in black and Chicano communities to create a dependency on heroin and undercut political movement.'

"According to the Rev. James Francek, associate pastor of the Cathedral of Detroit, 'This explosion of heroin has taken place only since 1967. In 1967 we had a revolution in this city and a lot of damage was done. The 1967 Detroit riot, the worst of all modern American civil disorders, left more than 40 dead and hundreds of millions of dollars lost in real estate and projected city business for that year. If you wanted to control people's minds, it would seem quite helpful if you had these people on a drug they were very much dependent on. Right after the riot one pusher said, "The police dried up the marijuana supply and they brought in junk, and its been here ever since." Despite some recent dramatic press accounts of heroin overdose deaths in the white middle-class suburbs, the Detroit heroin epidemic strikes poor black people most heavily. I can name ten people who O.D.'d (overdosed) and I bet you they haven't been heard about in the newspapers at all. But I read in the newspapers about one white guy overdosing out in Grosse Pointe (a wealthy, all-white suburb) and now there's some attempt to stop the heroin—at least in that community. I mean why don't they do it when all these black people are down here in the morgue from overdoses of drugs? Why?'

"The number of addicts in New York City alone went in 1967 from 90,000 to its present level of 400,000. In effect the heroin epidemic is relatively new and the timing of it seems too perfect to be dismissed as mere coincidence." That the epidemic is politically inspired is suggested by many of the facts now emerging about the heroin trade:

"The great bulk of heroin entering the U.S. comes from opium, not grown in Turkey, but in U.S. controlled regions of Indochina. Opium production in those U.S. controlled regions of Indochina increased *tenfold* from 1960 to 1970, much of it under the direction of CIA controlled mercenaries and transported by the CIA's Air America fleet. Even Myles Ambrose, head of the Justice Department's Office for Drug Abuse Law Enforcement admits that 'from 1961 to 1971 there has been a tenfold increase in the number of addicts.'

"Since 1966 the traditional heroin distribution system in the U.S. changed when the Mafia handled heroin in undisputed hegemony. The Mafia's settled harmony with big city police was disrupted in the mid-sixties by lapses of cooperation and local arrests and by high-level Federal prosecution of Mafia kingpins. Now much of the heroin traffic, at least along the East and Gulf Coasts, is ultimately controlled by anti-Castro Cuban refugees with CIA connections. Remember, it was the CIA who staged the Cuban Bay of Pigs fiasco which helped create much of the refugee problem. According to *The New York Times*, 'Among those who have moved into the drug trade are certain members of the ill-fated Assault Brigade 2506, which landed at the Bay of Pigs on April 17, 1971. Trained by the CIA, defeated on the Cuban beaches, ransomed by the U.S. government, some of these Cubans went into drug trafficking, putting to profitable use their newly learned guerrilla techniques.'

"Thus the government's control of Indochina's opium growth and its control of local distribution was effected during the years when ghetto rebellions were spreading and when opium production in Indochina was rapidly stepped up.

"With the great increase in the number of addicts, there has been a concomitant increase in the number of addict committed crimes. This increase in the number of crimes has been used as an argument for police forces to expand enormously, to function in the ghettoes as occupying armies, and to organize and affiliate for independent political power—in spite of the fact that very few addicts commit crimes of violence. The addicts tend to be sneak thieves, shoplifters, and lush rollers. To the extent that the present balances and policies of power in this nation at least appear to depend on wide and spreading heroin use by the blacks, particularly young blacks, our military involvement in Indochina is as much for the sake of heroin as for tungsten and oil. In brief there is considerable evidence, of at least a circumstantial nature, to suggest that heroin is being used by the government as an instrument of social control of the ghettoes."

Other malcontents are drugged into control by many of our most important institutions, so it shouldn't be surprising that it occurs against our most malcontented—those in the ghetto.

What about the malcontents outside the ghetto? Well, 10 percent of the adult population are alcoholics, that is, unhappy people subjugated by alcohol. The medical profession is bought by the pharmaceutical industry to calm discontented people by teaching them to pop pills, to tranquilize away their fears, worries, and concerns—legitimate or otherwise. The highest commercial art of the culture is used to persuade people to seek chemical remedy for social reality. Massive populations of children are legally drugged with amphetamines by school administrators to "adjust" them to schools rapidly growing more intolerable.

Rossman continues, "Historically it is well to remember that destructive drugs are a traditional tool of American policy, for deliberate cultural genocide. For example, the Opium Wars which opened the Orient to U.S. imperialism ended in an American 'victory' with *America's requiring China to legalize opium trade* [emphasis added], that is, forcing China to end its ban on the importation of opium." According to the Committee of Concerned Asian Scholars, "since 1729 Chinese laws prohibited the sale and smoking of opium, but American imperialism ended that ban. By 1839 so many Chinese had become addicts that China's desperate government destroyed 20,000 chests of opium. Western imperial forces promptly declared war, the first Opium War. The white man had declared war upon someone who objected to being narcotized." Of course the more Chinese were narcotized and addicted, the more the Chinese were forced to import opium and export cash in exchange, thereby shaking the Chinese fiscal system to its roots, not to mention its political, social, and cultural system.

Naturally, some of the Chinese rebelled. The leader of the rebelling Taipings said to their followers, "The opium pipe is like a rifle pointed at your head. It can only maim or kill you"—not much different from what ghetto leaders are telling their people.

Again according to the Committee of Concerned Asian Scholars: "American clipper ships ran opium to China. Opium was central to the rapid development of the American economy and the earliest stages of U.S. expansion into Asia. Major New England family fortunes were built on opium. One such family, the Delanos, later helped lift Franklin Delano Roosevelt to the presidency. American money made in the opium trade also helped finance the railroads that opened the American west which had been controlled by Indians."

Opium had done its work well. By first forcing China to import opium, the opium produced an addicted and therefore controlled population. The population was controlled to the point where the Chinese themselves were forced to grow the opium, but under Western control, thereby saving Western forces the cost of transporting the opium. By the early twentieth century American and other Western merchants had used money made in the opium trade to seize control of other key sectors of the Chinese economy. China was an addicted colony of non-whites until the successful revolution in 1949 established the People's Republic of China.

Michael Rossman comments:

"Before China, we used alcohol in a similar way with the Indians (Native Americans). Now in Harlem pushers deal heroin to eight-year-olds from white Cadillacs parked in front of the grammar schools, and liberals put the Panthers down for being paranoid and starting new 'Opium Wars.'"

Black Panther and former addict Michael Tabor calls heroin a "plague of epidemic proportions in the black community, and still growing. Despite supposedly stiffer jail sentences that are being meted out to those whom the law defines as being 'drug profiteers,' and that term is nothing but a euphemistic way of saying 'illegal capitalists,' there are more dope dealers now than ever before. Despite the increasing number of so-called rehabilitative and preventative programs, the plague proliferates and threatens to devour an entire generation of youth. Capitalism plus heroin equals genocide." Tabor notes that, "The basic and fundamental reason why the heroin plague cannot be stopped by the drug prevention and rehabilitation programs is that these programs, with their middle-class, archaic Freudian approach and group therapeutic concepts do not deal with the ultimate root causes of the problem. These programs deliberately negate the politico-economic origins of drug addiction. These programs sanctimoniously deny the fact that capitalistic exploitation and racial oppression are the main contributing factors to drug addiction. Since the programs are funded by the rulers of the capitalistic system, the programs could never be geared to turn the people against the ruler's system.

"These programs were never intended to seriously cure the black addict. The reactionary government of the U.S. defines the *cause* of addiction as the importation of the heroin plague into the country by dope smugglers. The government then tries to stop addiction by increasing its police force to stop the smuggling. The government knows very well that the smuggling cannot be stopped, so maybe the additional police forces will be used in other areas of control, such as in the ghetto. By focusing our attention on dope smugglers the government hopes to divert our attention away from the true causes that underly drug addiction. The government is well aware of the fact that even if they were able to stop the importation of heroin, dope dealers and addicts would just find another drug to take its place, perhaps a synthetic one, manufactured in underworld labs, obviating the need for smuggling.

"The government has no desire to address itself to the true causes of addiction, for to do so would necessitate making fundamental and basic institutional and structural changes. These changes could not take place, they could not possibly be effected without changing the manner in which property is owned and the manner in which wealth is distributed in this society. In short, only a revolution could eliminate this genocidal plague.

"The wretchedness of our plight, our sense of power-lessness and despair serve to create within our minds a predisposition and susceptibility towards the use of any element or substance that produces euphoria. We are strongly inclined to use anything that enables us to suffer peacefully, even if it's self-destructive. Our oppressor encourages our participation in any activity that is self-destructive.

"Our black people, especially our black youth, crave for euphoria, anything that will help to make them oblivious to the squalor, to the abject poverty, to the disease and degredation that engulfs them in their daily existence. And initially the white powdered plague does just that. Under its sinister influence the oppressive, nauseating ghetto prison is transformed into a virtual Valhalla. One becomes impervious to the rancid stench of urine-soaked tenement dungeons, unaffected by the piercing cries of anguish from black folks driven to the brink of insanity by our sadistic and predacious political system, unaffected by the deafening wail of police sirens as they tear through the streets of black hell en route to answer the call of some other police who are in a state of well-deserved distress, unaffected by the trash cans whose decayed, disease-carrying garbage has flowed over to fill the ghetto streets. Under heroin's ecstatic influence one becomes a full-time chartered member of the cloud-nine society and is made oblivious to the ugly social and political realities of life. And of course to stay on cloud nine the addict becomes physiologically and financially, psychologically and socially dependent on heroin and its pushers. The addict is buying death on the installment plan."

Just as the Western white man eventually forced the Chinese to grow their own opium, an analogous situation is occurring in our ghettoes. Because of the occasionally stiffer sentences meted out to pushers, major drug profiteers are gradually withdrawing from the lower levels of the market, "where the profits are smaller and the risks greater." Tabor points out that this has left a vacuum in the heroin market. A few years ago it was a rarity to find a black dope dealer who handled more than three kilos of heroin (one kilo equals 2 lb. 2 oz.) at any one time. Now blacks are filling that market vacuum, handling upwards of ten kilos of heroin. "Racists run the show, so the racial minorities not only take the risks but become bought off, become mercenaries in an army of destruction against their own people. In the occupied colony arrested, small-time addicts are coerced to become police spys, spying on their neighbors, looking for political agitators."

Under the guise of ridding the ghetto of dope, demagogic politicans on Capitol Hill passed a "no-knock" law which gives, as Tabor says, "narcotics agents a right to crash into a suspected dope dealer's house without knocking, if there is reason to believe that drugs may be destroyed. Now anyone who thinks that this law will be confined to just suspected dope peddlers is negating the fact that this country is becoming increasingly repressive, especially as its most oppressed people in all our ghettoes become more politically conscious. It should come as no surprise when the homes of revolutionaries and other progressive individuals are invaded by police under the pretext of searching for narcotics. A number of black revolutionaries have already been imprisoned on trumped-up narcotic charges, for example, Martin Sostre, sentenced to 41 years. You can rest assured that this policy will be intensified. When the police kick in a revolutionary's door, and crash through the windows with shotguns on the pretext of looking for drugs, they will find drugs because they bring them with them."

Also, *Medical World News* reports that "the Nixon Administration's no-knock drug control bill will sharply increase Attorney General Mitchell's men's power to inspect previously confidential physicians' records without warning."

With most addict's crime committed in the black community, after all a black would look pretty suspicious in an all-white community, the people of the black community have been duped into asking for more "police protection" and thus "more police are being deployed into the ghettoes, not for protection but for repression. It must be reiterated that the police have no desire to eliminate heroin" when they profit from it and in some ways are protected by it, because of its function as an agent of pacification and tranquilization.

Now it is no longer only the blacks who are threatened with the genocidal potency of heroin. Heroin is now afflicting the rebelling youth-street-freak ghettoes in much the way it does the black ghettoes. As Rossman notes, "In the youth ghetto, freaks and hippies are the white niggers of the counterculture. Their resemblance to the blacks has long been evident. They are hairy, sexy, looser, musical, etc.—and now the ravages of heroin in the black community are being repeated in the rebelling youth community."

As author Sol Yurick says, "Junkies do not band together in association and are therefore politically defused. Heroin is used to politically pacify the ghettoes, training youth to what is in effect a work ethic contrary to the cultural and social revolution they were seeking. The heroin work ethic provides the opportunity to erect a whole infrastructure of distributors, salesmen, and customers who have an ongoing investment and will themselves *work* to depoliticize, contain, co-opt and kill off those who threaten the market. Fifteen-year-old junkies are businessmen providing the one area where the young, trained for little at this point, can be brought into intensive economic behavior by becoming pushers."

The junk business has considerable parallels to the more socially acceptable forms of economic endeavor. The junk business is nevertheless a business, and its culture reflects a business or economic culture. For example, according to the Reverend Lynn Hageman, director of Exodus House, a New York drug rehab center, "If you ask a non-junkie on the street the question 'What are you?' the odds are that the response will be in terms of a vocational role or job. This has not always been true. Two generations ago you would have gotten an equal number of responses in terms of ethnicity, religion or even family name. The same change is noted in popular manners at cocktail parties where the introduction of strangers is immediately followed by production role identification. Two generations ago, by contrast, talking shop was considered to be bad form. If this caricature is at all true we ought not to be surprised or scandalized that rather large numbers of young people respond to a life-style identification in which they are someone in terms of a particular form of production. By this it may be inferred that the addict culture provides a production role identity rather quickly. The economic pressures are such that the serious drug user must find a business endeavor appropriate to his talents and opportunities. Thus the roles of shoplifter, drug seller, operator of a 'shooting gallery,' whore, pimp, etc., all meet the economic need or work ethic need of the addict, while at the same time giving rewards of status and identity, along lines of economic production, within the circle of peers whose esteem most matters. Economic and production skill is rewarded by recognition, and application and *perseverance* are acknowledged. Whether you are an ad-

dict or an ad man, you're a businessman that has to im-
press others. If you're an addict you have to show that you
have a terribly bad habit, which means that you are doing
a lot of good hustling, i.e., being a successful businessman.
Thus the profit ethic with its concomitant exploitation and
alienation is reproduced at all levels of society."

Rossman says that: "The white youth ghettoes were
forming during the mid-sixties, while the white student
movement was becoming a potential force for social
change. In 1967, their prototype, the San Francisco
Haight, was trumpeted nationally by the Media. Two
years later echo Haights were visible in 200 cities, and by
the early seventies many countercommunities were making serious bids for shares of civic power.

"Until the time of the Haight's exposure, the drug uses
of the San Francisco Bay Area countercommunity re-
volved almost exclusively around grass, LSD, and other
psychedelics. These drugs served many as powerful agents
of personal change, or spiritual and social insight, and
opened consciousness in a way compatible with *radical
social transformation* [emphasis added].

"Much of their manufacture and distribution were motivated in part by missionary zeal and humane concern;
and the drugs reached the people in *pure* condition and
with lore for their use as agents of growth.

"But from late 1966 on, a concatenation of events re-
organized most of the distribution system of psychedelic
drugs. Major dealers were murdered in many underworld
ways, some involving organized crime.

"Many neighborhood dealers were driven out by police
busts, by disruption of their supply, or by meeting a man
with a gun once too often. Police were efficient in perse-
cuting the freelance LSD manufacturers—especially those

who, like Owsley, made their drugs for community good as well as for profit.

"In 1967, when the activity generated in the Haight began to affect the whole city, all city agencies from building inspector on up cooperated to suppress it. And in that year, as the distribution system of psychedelics was being reshaped, contaminated psychedelics appeared for the first time in quantity in the Bay Area.

"First it was LSD, laced with speed or strychnine. In 1968 real THC appeared briefly, to whet public appetite, and then adulterated speed was massively peddled as THC to kids who had no idea of the difference, but took it because they'd been trained to do whatever was groovy.

"By 1969 the standard additives for LSD were speed and the animal tranquilizer PCP, with which it was marketed as mescaline—accounting for a major proportion of psychedelic use for the next several years, though almost no genuine mescaline was around.

"Wherever all the dirted drugs came from, they were eagerly peddled to the countercommunity by the Hip Capitalists.

"But Hip Capitalism is Capitalism still, in all its pristine ugliness under the psychedelic paint. They were interested mostly in quick profit in a high-turnover scene, and would sell almost anything to anyone without concern for what its broad effects would be.

"God damn the pusherman, especially when he calls himself 'brother.' For through his eager cooperation, ten million children of America have been conditioned to weird and destructive chemical body trips, and set well on the road to speed and heroin addiction.

"Junkies began showing up in the Haight in 1967, and speed and barbiturates started spreading through suburban high schools all over the nation. Matters took a sharp turn for the worse in 1969, the year after the Yippies appeared so dangerous in Chicago.

"During the Great Pot Drought of the summer, many people turned on to these drugs for the first time seriously —urged by a ready supply through new channels of organized crime, and by the widespread despair after Chicago and the death of the People's Park.

"During these years governments persecuted marijuana users unmercifully (there were 250,000 arrests in 1969), and mounted intensive border operations to interrupt supply, while policing the supply of heroin, speed and downers much less intensively.

"By such means the Official Line was that marijuana and heroin were equally evil. This misrepresentation was deeply political. Guided by its teaching and by blind antiauthoritarian reflex, many young people chose to treat all drugs with equal casualness, and suffered the consequence.

"By 1971 marijuana persecution seemed to be slackening, but the hook of heroin is deep in the countercommunity and junkies are dying along Telegraph Avenue in Berkeley. We know speed kills yet we keep on speeding anyway.

"And now the supply lines of these deadly drugs reach into the very place where the white young are conveniently gathered. From them a psychic numbness spreads, to reinforce the shock and warning of Kent State and Jackson State.

"As in the black ghettoes, the people turn criminal against themselves while police occupation spreads, and the youth potential for political action becomes undermined and corrupted. A cruel feedback begins: oppressed and politically impotent, the people turn to drugs to escape reality, and by self-destructive drug use deepen their impotence.

"One drug dependency can lead to another, and Hip Capitalism has been as instrumental as government policy in channeling psychedelic use into destructive drug addiction.

"The psychedelics are magical drugs. They can open up a genuine revolutionary awareness, help you get a sense of who you are and awaken you to the sickness that surrounds us. But once we've reached that awareness, we can't go home. Social reality is confused and painful these days, and sensitivity is agony as well as ecstasy.

"Either we push ahead and change the world, or else we fight our new awareness—with cynicism towards the world and pity for ourselves; by watering down our insights enough to fit in with the dominant social reality.

"Thus psychedelics are dangerous as well as magical. And grass will lead on to the numbness of heroin, as the old myths tell, unless we make it happen some other way."

As one Vietnam war veteran put it, "Drug addiction is the government's way of pacifying masses of young people. Just like in China, there will soon be an opium war here."

Community people, outraged at police and prosecution complicity and corruption, are now demonstrating and fasting on the doorsteps of police precinct stations. *The New York Times* reports that the 24th precinct in Manhattan has been a special target of community organizers. Groups have been marching in front of the station house chanting, "Police and the pusher work hand in hand, police and the pusher work hand in hand." The Upper West Side community "served" by the 24th precinct issued a statement printed in *The New York Times* which said in part: "While the public is aware of the efforts of the 24th precinct to create an image in this community of warmth and friendship, the public remains totally in the dark as to what the 24th is doing about the drug problem. We allege that they aren't doing a thing about it. We further allege that for the most part the heavy drug traffic exists *because the 24th precinct supports this traffic*" [emphasis added].

In Chicago, black vigilantes fed up with the failure of the local police to stop heroin traffic, are now "pushing the pushers." According to a *Newsweek* report of September 27, 1971: "The youthful drug pusher was slouching in his usual spot outside the O.K. Lounge in Chicago's West Side ghetto. Suddenly a dark blue auto slid to a stop at the curb and its driver—a 32-year-old black man named Hosea Lindsey—ordered the pusher over to the car. 'The next time you help someone in this neighborhood take dope,' Lindsey told him, 'I'm gonna beat your ass. And if you run, I'll chase you with a gun.' The pusher glanced from Lindsey to Lindsey's three scowling associates and then he began backing away from the car. 'OK, I won't do that any more,' he stammered." Then he walked quickly off as Lindsey and his friends exchanged satisfied looks.

Hosea Lindsey and his Afro-American Group Attack Team, a band of ten street-wise black vigilantes, thus scored another small victory. They have taken upon themselves the seemingly impossible mission of ridding their Chicago neighborhood of its Number One scourge, heroin. "We know we can't stop the use of heroin," allows Edward Mead, a 23-year-old member of the team, "but we think we can get junkies and dealers out of our community. Sure they'll move to another community, but maybe that community will organize and chase them out. Pretty soon they won't have any place to go but the river."

The beginning of the attack team had as much to do with vanity as it did with politics and community concern. In May 1971, Mead and Lindsey had their fanciest clothes stolen by a junkie. "All we had left was what was on our backs," Mead recalls. "We were mad . . . so we began beating up on junkies." Finally, Mead and Lindsey, both ex-convicts, organized a team to accomplish what the local police were unlikely, unable and unwilling even to attempt to do . . . making a start on ridding the community of heroin pushers.

The team began from a shabby building equipped with two cars and a mimeograph machine, and they first passed the word that pushers were now marked men. The team flooded the neighborhood with thousands of leaflets stating: "If you are caught selling heroin in this community, you will be in serious trouble." Then they organized daily street patrols, monitoring the pushers' favorite corners and threatening both pushers and dealers . . . often at gunpoint. To date the team has turned in twenty-one heroin pushers. Interestingly, the idea has spread; both the Italian and Spanish communities have organized similar groups.

All this has so disturbed the police that their district headquarters has launched an investigation of the black attack team, presumably to determine whether the vigilantes are in fact extorting money from the community they claim to be cleaning up. In response to this charge, the team accuses the police of fearing a decline in the area's heroin traffic, which would then reduce police graft and profits from narcotics trafficking. "The cops here take money from pushers," asserts Mead. "Every so often they bust a chump addict, but they do it just to keep their statistics up."

While it remains somewhat doubtful that these vigilantes can accomplish all they hope to, they do seem to be reaching the ghetto youth, while antagonizing the police and the Mafia. Lindsey notes that the big-time heroin dealers in the area have put a big price tag on his head.

When a group of concerned Manhattan Community College students began demanding administrative changes in the College in order to combat drug abuse, one College official responded, "They're all Maoists, Communists, and militant socialists, bent on destroying the American system. I wouldn't be surprised if they're involved in these cop-killings," he shouted, pointing to students raising complaints about the drug problem on the College's campus. For whatever solace it was worth, *The New York Times* supported the students' struggle.

Because these nonviolent vigilantes have had only a very limited degree of success in removing heroin from the community, William Rasberry, columnist for the *Washington Post*, reports that "the word is seeping through black ghettoes that vigilante action up to and including 'elimination' may be the only way to halt the growing use of heroin among black youths." Georgia black leader Julian Bond is now saying that "black people must let the sellers of poison to our children know that the price of heroin is death at the hands of the community." In the face of political, social, and cultural genocide it is hardly surprising that communities are arising in self-defense. As Dr. William Corson reported: Recently in Baltimore there were seven or eight pushers murdered. The effects of these killings by a "person or persons unknown" was that it was at least temporarily difficult to buy heroin in Baltimore and the supply of heroin in Baltimore had to be shifted to Washington, D.C. "It takes little imagination to realize that the elimination of pushers in this manner was most probably accomplished by black organizations, attempting to get the monkey off black people's backs. Obviously black militants cannot act directly against the growers and overseas transporters of heroin, but they can take direct action against the distributors. Black vigilantes may

be counted on to tackle the problem with the only immediate means at their disposal."

In the context of the antiheroin vigilante movement it
may be relevant to examine a specific case history:

Manhattan's Red Carpet Lounge on Eighty-fifth Street
is a drug drop "serving" the black and Puerto Rican cli-
entele at nearby Brandeis High School. Dealers line the
bar's front curb with shiny Cadillacs when making a delivery.

At the lounge on October 15, 1971, four men were
arrested and shot by the police for allegedly attempting
to rob the bar. One of the men shot was H. Rap Brown.
Since Brown went underground in April 1970, he has been
active in attempts to suppress heroin traffic, not in robbing
bars. At the time of his arrest and being shot, Brown and
his friends were threatening and demanding that the bar's
owners cease being a drug drop, or face judgment at the
hands of the community. The police were called in, not to
prevent a robbery, but to prevent Brown and the community from interfering with the heroin traffic pushed in
the area and profited from and protected by the police of
that neighborhood.

The community, which was quite well aware of Brown's
fight against heroin, honored Brown with the formation of
a formal organization called the H. Rap Brown Anti-Dope
Movement. The Movement is sponsored by a coalition of
groups represented by such people as Georgia politician
Julian Bond, Ms. Rosa Hamilton of New York's Welfare
Rights Organization, and Mamu Amire Baraka (LeRoi
Jones).

This Anti-Dope Movement plans to be a nationwide
coordinating group whose "primary goal is the elimination
of heroin from the black community by waging an aggressive campaign against pushers and suppliers. There

have been numerous incidents of mothers, fathers, friends and relatives who have taken it upon themselves to drive pushers and their so-called 'legitimate' fronts such as bars, restaurants, candy and 'variety' stores, florist shops, laundries and cleaning shops out of the black area. Because they have been alone in this struggle, rather than working on a community-wide basis, the impact of their work has had only a limited effect. Therefore we ask the aid and assistance of all sectors of the black community."

Julian Bond, who has been acting as spokesperson for the group, said that the group "would not only have its own surveillance, but its own tribunal and its own punishment." Bond said the group would use any means necessary to "eliminate people dealing in dope, from moral persuasion to more forceful deliberate means." Bond then quoted H. Rap Brown: "The price of dope is death."

Michael Tabor, Black Panther spokesperson, says that "the drug problem can only be dealt with by the residents of the ghetto. And the only manner in which they can do that is by organizing themselves into forces that will in effect harass, intimidate and if necessary, attack physically drug dealers. The dealers must be seen and dealt with for what they really are—enemies and murderers of the people. The dealers' actions and deeds, result in the destruction of the youth of our people. And we must understand that it is the youth who make the revolution. Without our young people we will never be able to forge and establish a powerful revolutionary force. We must understand dope for what it really is. It is a form of genocide in which the victim pays to be killed. If capitalism plus heroin equals genocide, then eliminate drugs by eliminating the cause of the drugs."

6 Law and Medicine: Professional Failures

The black and brown ghettos of our major cities are no longer the only areas of narcotics big business. As former New York City Police Inspector William P. Brown points out, increased campus interest in the direction of hard drugs is changing drug-trafficking patterns. The once relatively anarchistic distribution of dope in our youth ghettos is being challenged by the American heroin empire. New criminal organizations are coalescing around campus narcotics distribution. Narcotics peddling there "is no longer an informal matter which any young enterpreneur can blithely try for fun and profit. The hijacking of small-time youthful dealers has become common, and tough men —politically well protected—are beginning to emerge as the local campus distributors."

Brown also notes that the same decline in golden opportunities for ambitious youth is being noted in amateur narcotics smuggling. "Increasingly the youngster who goes abroad to buy dope that promises great profit has about an equal probability of being ripped-off by organized crime as he does by organized cops. In either case the

107

chances are good that the individual youthful smuggler was spotted on a tip from the seller." Brown says that "competition between cops and criminals for such information is brisk enough that whether the lone traveler in contraband winds up in a Tijuana alley or in an official's car is largely a matter of the economics of information. The lesson is clear: the day of the individual amateur dealer is over and the push is towards corporate narcotics organization."

Well, where does all this leave us in terms of diplomatic, military, and police control of heroin? Internationally, the CIA transports heroin; nationally, federal agents protect it, and locally, metropolitan police push it. Clearly, the attempt at controlling heroin through illegalization has only created more law-breakers . . . and an expanding heroin empire.

The history of illegalization of opium and opium derivatives, i.e., first opium, then morphine, and then heroin, has been a disastrous and tragic one. For example, opium, while addicting, is only mildly so, leaving one with a manageable habit. Smoking opium tends to promote conviviality and is usually smoked in groups. However, law enforcement agents were able to crack down easily on opium users and pushers because the smoke is very distinctive and thus has a detectable aroma. Pushers and addicts then turned to morphine, which was subsequently outlawed. Morphine is more addicting and less socializing than opium. Moreover, it cannot be compacted as well as heroin, and thus is not as easy to smuggle. Consequently, the market was ripe for heroin. Heroin is easy to concentrate highly and thus is easy to smuggle. Because it is usually taken intravenously, there is no distinctive odor associated with it. Worse, however, is the fact that heroin is a highly alienating and one of the most addicting drugs known. Thus illegalization has forced the drug market to evolve from the socializing and mildly addicting drug, opium, to the alienating and highly addicting heroin.

If illegalization has been a failure, then what about legalization of heroin? What are some of the advantages of legalizing heroin? Legalization would eliminate heroin as a social problem and relegate it to a more personal one. First of all, 50 to 75 percent of all crime committed in our metropolitan areas, according to the Vera Foundation, is perpetrated by heroin addicts each stealing three hundred to five hundred dollars' worth of goods a day to support, from the resale of those goods, a forty- to fifty-dollar-a-day habit. A half million addicts doing this much stealing is a multibillion-dollar crime bill, not to mention the expenses of law enforcement, prisons, insurance, etc.

The high cost of heroin, secondarily to its illegalization, has led many women addicts to turn to prostitution just to meet survival expenses. In a sexist society it is difficult for a woman to earn adequate amounts of money except as a sex object. Almost 50 percent of all New York City prostitutes are addicts. Prostitution, of course, is one of the major sources of spread of venereal disease.

Charles Winick in his *The Lively Commerce* reports that "as many as 90 percent of all professional prostitutes are infected with venereal disease at some time during their career, and each prostitute can infect an average of twenty men before her disease is discovered."

A San Francisco public health research project showed that a prostitute can infect fifty to seventy-five men within one month.

So that as the price of heroin goes up because of any "successful" law enforcement efforts, more and more women addicts turn to prostitution, which in turn adds significantly to the VD epidemics sweeping the country.

In a somewhat reversed situation many pimps have been instrumental in encouraging addiction in their prostitutes. The addiction is encouraged so that the women are constantly in need of money and thus more willing to be prostitutes.

Given the occupational oppressiveness of prostitution, many women find that heroin calms them and enables them to tolerate their work. Some prostitute addicts have noted that heroin makes it easier for them to have anal intercourse because the drug relaxes the anal sphincter muscles. According to Charles Winick, virtually no prostitutes have felt that heroin interfered with their ability to perform for clients. Inasmuch as it is nearly impossible to detect the presence of heroin in a user by nonlaboratory methods, only an experienced and sophisticated client is likely to be aware of her drug use.

An addict prostitute's customers are not the only men who "use" her. Winick points out that law enforcement agencies routinely use addict prostitutes as informers, with the understanding that they will receive special consideration in sentencing. A New York City judge admitted recently that, "Certainly we parole the women for this purpose. It is not a nice business. An addict prostitute who has been arrested is likely to be lonely and harassed. When she needs some hope of rehabilitation she is offered help—but only on the condition that she become an informer and contribute to the arrest of her friends and former associates. Forcing a woman into such morally and ethically compromising situations is hardly likely to aid in her rehabilitation."

The laws against prostitution are ultimately a factor in prostitutes' becoming addicts. First of all, the enforcement of the laws are discriminatory on the basis of sex, class, and race. It is the women who are arrested, not the men.

Middle-class white women, with access to some jobs and money, are more likely to be "call girls," higher paid, less linked to pimps, and highly unlikely to be arrested. Conversely, it's the poor black woman with little access to jobs or money who is tied to a pimp, walking the street, and highly susceptible to arrest. The law encourages the arrest of these susceptible women. As Pamely Roby, sociologist at Brandeis University, points out, "once the woman is arrested and lacking money for bail she is forced to rely on her pimp, reinforcing her financial and often drug dependency. By being labeled as criminals the women lose whatever chance they may have for 'respectable' jobs, keeping them in constant contact with pimps, pushers, and other addicts. The only other line of work a prostitute can get into is as a pusher." Professor Roby concludes, "Sexism, racism and class inequality shape the lives of these women and limit their options to prostitution and pushing."

With so much of our crime and corruption, death and disease directly related to heroin's illegalization, when one hears a politician promising to do something about "crime in the streets" or "law and order," unless that politician is planning to deal seriously with heroin, you know he's whistling in the wind and/or is a demogogue.

Legalized heroin maintenance is very cheap. Pure heroin to support a daily habit would cost only a few cents a day. On the other hand, President Nixon's token methadone treatment and rehabilitation program is a multibillion-dollar program. The *initial* aspects of the program, during the program's first three years, will cost, according to an Associated Press report of March 15, 1972, over one billion dollars from the federal government alone, and worse, appears doomed to failure, as will be explained below.

First of all, methadone is itself addicting. Methadone

was originally synthesized, perhaps not surprisingly, by the German firm I. G. Farben, in 1941, for Nazi Germany as a replacement for morphine. Historically, it must be remembered that heroin originally appeared before the American public as a "treatment" for opium and morphine addiction, in much the same way that methadone does now, i.e., supposedly to "treat" heroin addiction.

Many U.S. troops near the turn of the century had become addicted to morphine following the introduction of the syringe. Morphinism became so common among veterans that it was referred to as "the soldier's disease." By 1913 heroin was well on its way as a treatment for morphinism among thirty soldiers at Fort Strong, Massachusetts. The U.S. Surgeon General at that time, in the official journal, *Military Surgery*, "desired to acquaint medical officers with the potential addicting nature of heroin with the possibility of it spreading beyond a few troops," although he "considered such a condition as highly improbable!"

Methadone has received a lot of support from so-called experts who claim that the methadone addict is supposedly able, within limits, to function as a normal person. As Dr. William Corson points out: "Evidence to support this assumption is indirect: heroin addicts have been able to meet the *social worker's criterion* of success, to take a job." However, little if any research has been done into whether the methadone addict can function in a job commensurate with his/her heroin capacity. Can he/she endure the emotional stresses that heroin allowed them to endure more effectively than methadone. That is, methadone may make a person less socially and politically functional, not more.

As Morris H. Bernstein, M.D., of Mount Sinai School of Medicine, points out: "Methadone used in treatment programs lacks heroin's effectiveness in giving pleasure and is far less effective than heroin in reducing anxiety or depression or as an anti-psychotic agent." To take it a step further, as Dr. William Corson points out, "He who controls the dispensation of methadone has the means to control the patient." For example, a group of revolutionary ex-addicts known as White Lightning spoke of the controlling aspects of the methadone maintenance program: "They build you up gradually to 180 milligrams so that if you shoot up heroin it wouldn't affect you. They can keep you at that level for the rest of your life. The whole idea of maintenance is to keep you up there like a robot. So they keep total control over you at all times, because you need that methadone fix and there ain't no way, if you were up there at 180 milligrams, that any kind of heroin or street drug is gonna take care of you. We feel that methadone has important political implications aside from the fact that the dosage that's given to people is higher than any other kind of drug. It's like chemical fascism. See, they *do* care about whether you stay on or stay off. They don't want you to get off."

Another member of White Lightning with a criminal record was given an alternative by the government: "State prison or take probation in a methadone program. Naturally, I took the methadone program. They didn't care whether I got a job or nothing. They just wanted me to stay on methadone where you're under their control. They know they got you then. Methadone is worse than heroin in a lot of ways, especially in terms of the long-range political implications. We realize that what the city is doing and what the government is doing is building an army, an army of zombies, strung out on methadone. And as soon as a political group or movement of people who really want to bring about some change in this country starts to move, those zombies can very easily be turned loose on them. The government will say, 'Well, if you want your methodone, you'd better go crack skulls.' Revolutionaries like ourselves have traditionally ignored the drug problem and what it means. What happens historically is that people like addicts and criminals turn out to be fascist thugs. Unless we reach these people first, there's going to be a group of people who should be on our side that are going to be against us."

Thus the physical control of methadone can be used by program administrators to force black patients to conform to white establishment standards of behavior. For example, New York's Health Policy Advisory Center reported that as early as May 1970, in one of the City's methadone maintenance programs, all patients were required to remove any political buttons before they would be allowed to receive their methadone.

Corson notes that politicians who control methadone funds do understand the political implications of such control and "can be counted on to use that power for political purposes. We don't even have to look to the future for oppression in the program. Take a look at the Federal Government's new regulations about methadone. Administrators of methadone programs are required to maintain detailed case histories on addicts, which literally force the addict to incriminate him or herself by confessing when, where, in what circumstances and how long he/she has been on heroin. The addict may be turned away if he/she fails to provide the required background information. The regulations also compel him/her to submit to follow-up surveillance and reporting on conditions not unlike those imposed on a parolee." The control of subsequent behavior of black ex-heroin addicts can hardly be perceived simply as "benign neglect." Corson continues: "All in all, the temptation to use methadone treatment programs as more than the means to aid afflicted persons is too real to be ignored." Good intentions are not enough "when power is at stake." As a recent case in point, "the actions of Clark Mollenhoff, the ex-White House aide who was able to get so-called 'confidential' Internal Revenue Service information on persons of interest to the White House, produced loud outcries from Congress. Would there be a similar Congressional outcry if heroin addicts' records were made available to those concerned with the social effect of heroin addiction, such as the police and welfare organizations?"

A survey conducted by *The New York Times* of fourteen major American cities that have methadone maintenance programs has found that in all of them there is illegal trafficking in the synthetic, addicting drug, methadone. As methadone has gained popularity as a clinical alternative to heroin, it nevertheless has joined heroin on the streets as a black-market commodity. The *Times* reports that "both the supply of and demand for methadone is growing."

The supply has several origins: outpatients on methadone maintenance programs who sell part of their allotted dose to purchase heroin for themselves, thefts of methadone from pharmacies and methadone maintenance programs, by both addicts and employees, and a small number of private physicians who prescribe an overgenerous quantity of the drug, which then finds its way into the black market.

Gene Haslip, special assistant to the director of the Bureau of Narcotics and Dangerous Drugs, said that almost every city in the country has at least one doctor or maintenance program that produces an important diversion of methadone into the black market.

Underworld elements have already opened their own methadone laboratories. As early as two years ago federal agents arrested one underworld chemist for the illegal manufacture of methadone.

The principal customers for black-market methadone are heroin addicts. They stockpile the drug to tide themselves over Sundays, "when you can't rip off your pork chops," i.e., steal from closed stores. Addicts also mix it with the diluted heroin sold in America to achieve a more potent "high." Addicts also "cop meth," i.e., steal it or buy it illegally when heroin is not available on the streets. Other customers for black-market methadone are found in the rapidly growing population of polydrug abusers who swallow, "shoot up," or "snort" a wide variety of legal and illegal drugs.

The New York Times investigative reporter James Markham reports that "the price of illegally obtained methadone varies from city to city—even within sections of one city—but it is usually cheaper than heroin, enabling a heroin addict "to relax a bit from hustling or taking care of business." In New York, Minneapolis, or New Orleans, a thirty-dollar-a-day heroin addict can satisfy his "drug hunger" with five to ten dollars' worth of methadone—forty to eighty milligrams. In Miami, the price might be twice as high, in San Diego even higher.

Dr. Vincent Dole, who pioneered the development of methadone maintenance, said "that in part, the considerable black market for methadone was a reflection of the inadequacies of methadone programs."

There is a growing number of methadone-related deaths round the country. Of the fourteen cities surveyed by *The New York Times*, all have had methadone-related deaths. Minneapolis had thirteen "proven" methadone deaths. The new slums in Westchester County in New York recently reported nine deaths from methadone.

"In the first two months of this year, New York City and the District of Columbia—which have the two largest methadone-maintained populations in the country—have had more methadone overdose deaths from the drug than in the previous twelve months. The Washington statistics are particularly striking because for the first six weeks of 1972, methadone has been almost as lethal as heroin in the nation's capital."

In addition to the addicts killed by methadone, is the large number of young children being poisoned, occasionally fatally, by the drug. Dr. Regine Aronow of Children's Hospital of the University of Michigan notes that for children "the number of admissions for methadone poisoning exceeds that for barbiturates and tranquilizers combined. Methadone is one of the few drugs that can fatally poison a toddler with one pill."

As methadone programs are expanding, so is the illegal diversion of methadone, creating more and more legal *and* illegal methadone and methadone-heroin addicts. As with heroin, the death rate from methadone will rise year after year, with the only effect being the creation of new, more, and younger addicts, as the illegal diversions continue. The clinics will usually dispense the methadone in plastic vials mixed with orange or grape Tang which, with some mild distilling, is injectable. The other method of clinic dispensing is with the Lilly Company's "Disket," which can be dissolved in water and rendered suitable for injection.

As investigative reporter Walter Anderson noted: "The aura of legitimacy surrounding methadone has created in Westchester County alone more than 100 methadone addicts out of people who wouldn't have touched heroin. Methadone is available in methadone clinics and sold on the street. Many addicts steal an extra bottle if they can from the clinic. Why? In order to buy 'Coke' (cocaine) which doesn't show up in the methadone clinics' urine testing program. One addict says that methadone has made Coke popular again, particularly when taken in combination or in tandem with methadone."

According to Dr. Karst Besteman of the National Institute of Mental Health: "The re-emergence of cocaine is one of the new clear trends in the murky picture of drug abuse in America, in part because of the increasing use of methadone. Cocaine exerts its powerful stimulant action even in the presence of methadone and/or heroin in the body. Therefore a heroin addict, under treatment with methadone and desperate for any kind of high or euphoria, might try cocaine. The addict would not be able to get a satisfying effect from heroin because methadone blockades the effect of heroin. Thus methadone, rather than eliminating the market for an illegal drug, e.g., heroin, is in fact creating a market for an additional illegal drug, cocaine.

"Methadone is a dangerous drug, in fact it's an experimental drug. It's not secretly shipped in from Marseilles, but created in legitimate labs here and funded by the public through tax dollars."

Community health workers who used to say to "speed freaks," i.e., people addicted to amphetamines such as methadrine, "Don't mess with meth," are now saying the same thing about methadone.

Secondly, methadone as a treatment will fail because of the fact that addicts take and are attracted to heroin because it creates a sense of euphoria, which methadone, at least according to some "experts," doesn't. Since the overwhelming majority of addicts started and stayed in the lowest economic strata, started and stayed unemployed and haven't much to look forward to, their lives won't be substantially improved by changing from heroin to "noneuphoric" methadone, other than the fact that the addicts will not have to steal for their methadone supply, that is, assuming the addict can get into one of the hugely overcrowded methadone programs.

In New York City, the waiting time for admission to a methadone treatment program is up to two years, according to the *New York Law Journal*, during which time addicts are forced to continue to rely on the illegal black market for heroin and/or methadone.

It is precisely for this fact of cutting down on stealing and crime, rather than curbing addiction or helping addicts, that Nixon is pushing methadone, rather than doing anything substantive about the causes of addiction, e.g., poverty, racism, etc. . . . If poor people take to heroin for the euphoria it creates, they may not have much to cheer about on "noneuphoric" methadone . . . and thus at least considerable numbers of methadone clients won't take it for very long and will revert back to heroin, as seems to be indicated by the statistics now being reported.

A recent report appearing in the *Journal of the American Medical Association* showed that only 5 percent of the methadone client group under study was considered improved by methadone, i.e., not reverting back to heroin. The study implied that even this group of 5 percent would not be considered "improved" if they were to be evaluated a year later. The study noted that "many patients who are admitted for methadone treatment primarily on the basis of a *history* of addiction may not be addicted, but rather may be only occasional users. Thus there is the danger of turning this group into hard-core methadone addicts," where "successful" treatment of the "addict" may be the production of a methadone addict out of a nonaddict.

The *Journal* editorialized about the study: "One can

discern an alarming inclination to view the drug, methadone, as a simple, inexpensive answer to the problem of
heroin addiction. Such an opinion creates a powerful
pressure for hasty, large-scale, underfinanced, and ill-con-
sidered programs." For example, New York's Mayor Lindsay recently announced plans to triple the City's methadone services. As Robert Newman, M.D., director of the
Methadone Maintenance Treatment Program for New
York City, admits: "Methadone cannot solve the community's addiction problem. It is absolutely impossible, no
matter how many or types of methadone programs exist
or what their capacity is."

On the other hand, if methadone does produce some
euphoria similar to heroin, as some addicts (i.e., addicted
to heroin and/or methadone) and physicians maintain,
then methadone is not significantly different from heroin,
except that it can be legally and medically dispensed,
which is why so many physicians, politicians, and community leaders oppose it, believing, in all likelihood correctly, that methadone is a legalized form of synthetic
heroin.

According to author and ex-addict William Burroughs:
"Many doctors prescribe methadone for addicts. They say
addicts lose the desire for heroin in the course of this
treatment. Over a period of five years they hope to reduce
the dosage of methadone, which is an opiate stronger
than morphine and quite as addictive. To say that addicts
have been cured by the use of methadone is like saying an
alcoholic has been cured of whiskey by the use of gin. If
the addicts lose their desire for heroin it is because the
methadone dosage is stronger than the diluted heroin they
receive from pushers."

According to Dr. Mitchell S. Rosenthal, "methadone,
crushed, cooked and injected gives the addict a greater,

more euphoric high than heroin. When the quality of street heroin is deteriorated, addicts look for methadone."

To find an alternative to the "synthetic" heroin, i.e., methadone, problem, with its addicting and apparent euphoric qualities, millions of dollars of public monies are now being spent on the development of a nonaddictive, noneuphoric heroin replacement or a drug which will block the craving for heroin.

With a lot of federal and local money available, Defense contractors and pharmaceutical corporations are increasingly working hand-in-hand to grab new sources of income in the search for a noneuphoric "heroin antagonist."

Dr. James Adams, a spokesman for the Pharmaceutical Manufacturers Association (PMA), said on November 22, 1971, that "the Defense Department has developed potent chemical warfare drugs that might be used to fight addiction." Adams declared that "when the Pentagon developed chemical warfare agents it usually also developed an 'antagonist' drug as an antidote for the protection of its own forces. It is such an antagonist that the pharmaceutical industry is now seeking and believes may be hidden in the secret results of Defense Department research."

Already at least nine drug companies are at work on a heroin antagonist as addicted veterans are coming back to civilian society. The specter of their addiction is used as a ploy by drug companies to ply federal money loose for their corporations' profitable research. As one administrator put it, "Drug abuse treatment is an expanding fiscal rubric." In perspective it must be recalled that the pharmaceutical industry has in the last twelve years always been among the top three most profitable corporations in the country.

New York City itself has funded and paid for a quarter-of-a-million-dollar study of the noneuphoric, heroin antagonist, drug, cyclazocine. Unfortunately, the City will be left holding the bag. Heroin addicts take heroin because they want to feel euphoric.

Heroin antagonists such as cyclazocine or naloxone will fail precisely because they block the euphoria of heroin. Whether or not the heroin antagonist is long acting is irrelevant to the addicts' goals of euphoria. And given the vast market demands for euphoric drugs, underground and/or criminal laboratories will simply develop new euphoric agents not blocked by heroin "antagonists." As one chemist put it: "For every antagonist discovered we can synthesize three new powerful euphoric-producing drugs. It's like the arms race or missile race; ICBM's are countered with ABM's which in turn are countered by anti-ABM's, which in turn sets off a new cycle. War can't be stopped by building more missiles any more than addiction can be stopped by making more 'antagonists.'"

When drug abuse psychotherapy treatment centers insist that ". . . the key to treatment of the addict is to turn the addict on to life," they fail to understand that most addicts are perceiving their life realistically, i.e., seeing and feeling the oppressive poverty, racism, and sexism of their daily lives, and are thus looking for available alternatives . . . of which euphoric-producing drugs are one such alternative.

Author Sol Yurick, in his economic analysis of heroin, comments on the use of psychotherapy in drug abuse treatment programs:

"There is a fantastic rise in the therapy market. Theories of addiction-cause and its cures proliferate. Studies are financed. Pilot projects are funded. New jargons develop. Again each psycho-social theory of the cause and cure of the habit doesn't have to be valid: what is valid is the ability to sell the theory, to get funding for the theory, to convince some legislator and possibly addicts that the program works, to demonstrate some successes, and to generate in the wake of failures still further programs. Social scientists compete fiercely in the open-program market for funding, and competition is the spur to the growth of a body of scientific capital: the point is to get that program on the market first and sell it. This has also given rise to a new job category. The professional junkie who goes from program to program getting funds to keep alive, demonstrating the success of each program. In its wake a large apparatus of doctors, social workers, counselors, reformed junkies, lecturers, psychiatrists, writers of books and articles (myself included), psychologists, political, administrative, clerical, police, and judicial jobs is created, as well as a mode of job retraining for a whole body of social and poverty workers whose situation is threatened by massive cutbacks in the poverty programs.

"Ex-addict and now director of a California drug therapy program, Ernie DiGiacomo, said in *Behavior Today* that 'Drug addiction means money—for dealers, wholesalers, smugglers, fences, officials on the take. Now, with massive funding of drug abuse programs, addiction means money for others—researchers, therapists, administrators, consultants, pharmaceutical houses, urinalysis labs. The vultures—those people who hang around waiting for a quarter to drop out of your pocket—are really into it. The same things that made me take dope to begin with are geting me and others into the drug abuse business.' Ex-addict and now director of a drug abuse program in New York, Frank Garcia says in a published interview that he 'could earn $100,000 a year if he hired himself out as an expert consultant to the Federal Government, the Board of Education, or some local communities starting a drug

program.' And many of these people, being in key positions to see economic possibilities, break their bureau-
cratic/professional relations in this therapy apparatus and
enter the market as pushers and middlemen.

"The therapy rites in addict cure have taken their lead
from the techniques evolved by Alcoholics Anonymous, a
variant of Christian Redemption, built around the con-
cept that addiction reflects certain inherent psychological
instabilities and character deformations. The pattern is
familiar: the weakness, the temptations, the self-indul-
gence, the rise and fall and the redemption through recognition and perception of oneself as a child of original sin.
To be sure, these weaknesses are spoken of in psychological rather than in traditional Christian terms, but the
whole Christian journey of self-degradation, self-negation,
the trip through hell, the public confession, the self-abase-
ment, the blinding insight, the revival and the salvation
is evoked."

As for the Protestant work ethic, Donald Miller of the
Federal Bureau of Narcotics and Dangerous Drugs points
out that the ultimate economic goal of eliminating narcotics by its illegalization and/or concomitant therapy
programs is reasonable because "We have accepted industriousness as a way of life. Like two other countries, Japan
and Germany, we emphasize resources and productivity.
Any time something encroaches on our industriousness we
have a right to impose our will on those who become a
threat to our way of life, who reduce our productivity."

Parenthetically, in what must be the ultimate perversion
of therapy and psychiatry, psychiatrist Dr. Donald Has-
tings, chairman of the Department of Psychiatry of the
University of Minnesota, says that "heroin addicts tend to
be rendered impotent by moderately high levels of heroin." Therefore it has been suggested by some psychia-

trists that "enforced morphine or heroin addiction be used upon recidivist sexual psychopaths such as rapists to render them impotent."

Therapists may have humanitarian instincts, but this tends to be contradicted by their technical training, which presupposes certain political investments that may be at variance with one's humaneness. At least if the therapists were radical therapists and admitted that psychological science doesn't exist independently of a political position, the radical therapist might suggest a *desirable political* context in which to be a junkie. For example, show the addict how and where to steal so that each theft is a political attack on the system that creates the junkie.

"But the therapy of addicts aims to reintroduce the *need*, if not to abstain, to at least self-regulate one's hungers, to introduce planning and long-range goals, to forego euphoria."

The failure of psychotherapy for the addict, even by conventional criteria, was evidenced in a report from the American Psychiatric Association which gave the example of a psychotherapeutic community "in which 40 percent of the addicts who had been offered admission to the therapy program as an alternative to a jail sentence subsequently asked to be returned to jail!"

Cyclazocine, methadone, or even psychotherapy are hardly viable alternatives to heroin or to racism and poverty.

The Vera Institute of Justice notes that in spite of all the above-mentioned programs "many of our most troubled addicts are not being reached by such programs. They either refuse voluntarily to enter treatment or have dropped out of these programs. A substantial portion of heroin addicts, including some of the most crime-prone, are unlikely to be reached by the simple expansion of any or all of the existing programs. According to Dr. Alfred M. Freedman, chairman of the Department of Psychiatry of New York Medical College: "All the heroin addiction treatment programs in New York City *combined* do not even begin to cope with the *City's* annual *increment* in the number of addicts, let alone the backlog," i.e., there is a backlog of now four hundred thousand addicts with an annual increment of around thirty-five thousand, in New York City alone.

Summarizing the efficacy of both law enforcement and medical-psychological treatment programs, federal attorney Whitney N. Seymour, Jr., presented the following data: "The Crime Analysis Section of the New York City Police Department conducted a study of persons arrested who admitted being heroin addicts. A majority of the arrested addicts had received narcotics treatment in hospitals and clinics and an even larger number had been previously arrested. The conclusion is unescapable that both our legal and treatment processes have made very little impact in reducing the demand for drugs by present heroin users. Every single treatment program which has not carefully pre-selected (i.e., selecting people who would probably cease to be addicts on their own, regardless of or in spite of a treatment program) its clients, has ended up with a failure rate of over 90 percent." The failure rate would undoubtedly have been much higher if the evaluations were carried over a longer period of time, and as more and more addicts inevitably dropped out of the treatment program.

7 The Addiction-Education-Industrial Complex

For those addicts who can't or won't be weaned away from heroin or satisfied by heroin substitutes, such as methadone, or heroin "blockers," such as cyclazocine or naloxone, or psychotherapy, "educational" programs are being developed to convert the "pagans." As social psychiatrist Dr. Seymour Halleck notes in his article, "The Great Drug Education Hoax," "The American people have a great faith in education." Educational institutions and their educational professionals have set out to educate our young people about heroin with a vengeance. Part of their motivation to push "education" comes from the numerous sources and great amounts of public monies now available for drug education.

For example, the U.S. Office of Education alone, which is only one of numerous federal, state, local, and private agencies involved in drug education, spent in the fiscal year 1971 over $13 million. Not unexpectantly, defense contractors who garnered the public's money spent for the war in Vietnam do not wish to miss out on new sources of governmental money. Thus major defense contractors who specialize in antipersonnel weaponry are now pushing and profiting from addiction education films, courses, programmed learning devices and literature. *Time* magazine recently revealed that at least "35 out of 85 such films and teaching aids were scientifically unacceptable and/or inaccurate."

One of the more humorous teaching programs designed by sociologists, mathematicians, and computer experts is a federally distributed, five-hour long, thirty-two-player "drug education simulation game," entitled Community at the Crossroads. The PR hype accompanying the game informs us that "A simulation is a representation of reality. Thus the Simulation Kit contains, among other paraphernalia, 32 police reports, a budget report and clergymen's report cards." The kit sells for only $13.75.

Such defense *and* "drug-education" corporations as American Telephone and Telegraph, Lockheed, Raytheon, and the 3M company emphasize, not the political, social, and economic roots of heroin addiction, but rather the establishment's ideology that heroin leads to the ruin of reputation, career, and property.

And Defense Department contractors are not the only corporations interested in this new drug-education money. Drug companies, such as Smith, Kline and French, which have legally pushed amphetamines ("speed") for years, are now becoming part of the American heroin empire by selling worthless addiction education literature. One of the drug company's salesmen, Dean Roberts, who is now teaching drug education in Jacksonville, Florida, admits that "I tell the kids that I was a pusher long before they were born." Roberts, now, instead of pushing drug addiction, is pushing drug education, but with essentially the same corporate mentality and priorities.

As one major drug company said, only half facetiously,

"Drug abuse is everyone's business—a very big business."

As Sol Yurick points out, drug companies aren't the only groups profiting from the pushing industry. "Millions have been invested in the purchase of sites deteriorated, decayed or deserted buildings for rehabilitation centers: architects and remodelers have been hired; By March 1970 one agency alone in New York had spent over $100 million for capital expenses for drug abuse buildings.

"While all New York City jails are crowded to the point of 160 percent of capacity, the best jail in the city, at 75 Morton Street, remains vacant following a six-million-dollar renovation construction job to house confined narcotics addicts. The removal of prisoners from this jail to others has in fact been a serious contributing factor to the overcrowding of the city's jails. The point is that money is going primarily for capital construction and not staffing. No money has been funded for staffing the facility, in spite of the fact that 70 percent of New York City prison inmates are addicts.

"Phantom, but paid-for, plans have been generated for centers that have not been built, and never will be. Ingenious black-market activities have sprung up: for instance, *clean* urine is sold to junkies who have to report to probation officers. The rise in the home-security market is stunning. Alarm systems, unbreakable locks and grates and chains are devised; dogs are bought; weaponry is purchased."

Elsewhere, in the February issue of the law-enforcement journal *Justice*, Universal Detective Inc. ran an ad beginning as follows:

> Extra agents when you need them. For large or small jobs. In the community, correctional institutions, industrial plants, on campus, in schools, many other situations. "*Rent-a-Narc!*"

According to the information the price is $230 a week (first and last week in advance) for four to thirteen weeks. The police department employing the agent would also pay for all drugs purchased.

The promotional material includes the following testimonial from the Chief of Police of Hampton, N.H.: "The last agent you sent to us was John Baum and in my opinion he was the best so far. I feel the work he did for us was outstanding in this ever ending [*sic*] battle. John was a real joy to work with and my detectives have the greatest regards [*sic*] for him."

It also included the following quote from *The International Narcotic Report*: "These agents undergo a basic training procedure to familiarize them with the different types of dangerous drugs and narcotics. They also undergo training where they are familiarized with the different types of slang that are used by pushers and users on the street . . . on one occasion, the agents had the pushers move into their cottage, where they would break up keys of marijuana, ounces of heroin and prepare them for distribution. Many of the small dealers and users in the area were arrested due to the efforts of these agents." Entrapment, anyone?

A new, uniquely American, and perhaps surprising source of addiction education is comic books. Not to be outdone by defense contractors and pharmaceutical houses, comic book publishers are plunging skin deep into the world of social relevance: the superhero as junkie.

Comic book publishers, faced with dipping sales, realized they couldn't make a buck with more of the same colorfully costumed superheros battling colorfully costumed superbaddies. So heros with hang-ups have been introduced, making the big switch from sleuth to smack (heroin).

The impact, if any, of this material is on young kids. For them it is an exposure to a harsh reality, an introduction to the nastiness of the seventies' civilization, to the fact that anyone . . . even the masculine, strong-minded, odorless stereotypical American hero . . . can become a victim of heroin.

While the story lines are woefully oversimplified, the political line is often correct, if not too general. For example, in the Green Arrow and Speedy comics, society is said to be sick and with dope the *symptom* of a sick society, not the disease itself. The big dealer is pictured as a dandied sophisticate with a pharmaceutical company on a Caribbean island as a business front. The dealer has a huge yacht that he packs with judges, senators, and beautiful women, mixing his pleasure cruise with a little business.

Unfortunately the reasons people take to heroin are skimmed over in the comic, though with a considerable grain of truth: minority and ethnic groups use it in reaction to the pain of racial prejudice. While this is undoubtedly true, the pain of racial prejudice is characterized simply as name-calling and dirty looks, rather than as a day-to-day fight for survival. The explanation for white kids shooting-up is "loneliness." Again, while this is true to a degree, it certainly oversimplifies and hardly explains why. Speedy in the comics has been taking to dope because Green Arrow has been ignoring him.

In the September 1971 issue of *Green Arrow*, Green Arrow is mugged by a gang of young "needle freaks" (addicts) who wind up shooting him with a crossbow. He crawls along the pavement. A swinging couple ignore him: "It's not smart to get involved, Mary." Green Arrow crawls to a phone booth. It's out of order. He creeps up to a cop writing a parking ticket. "Help me," says Green Arrow. "Go home and sleep it off, fella," says the cop. An empty taxi passes him up, flashing its off-duty light when he flags it. Finally he makes it to the emergency room of a hospital, where the nurse tells him they're too busy to treat him until morning. Green Arrow collapses on his desk, saying, "Isn't modern civilization wonderful?"

Unfortunately, it's all downhill from here. After a bunch of preachy asides, Green Arrow recovers and catches the baddies, but not without first being captured and shot full of heroin. Speedy kicks his habit in time, with the help of Green Arrow's girl friend (women play only supporting roles in these comics), to bail out Green Arrow and help in the final capture. Now that Green Arrow is full of heroin, there's no way of knowing who may be next.

Liberal educators have been congratulating *Green Arrow* comics on their "boldness in dealing with a terrible problem." And the November 1971 issue features a letter of praise from Mayor John Lindsay, whose own police and antiaddiction programs have done so remarkably little to combat heroin. Maybe he should hire a cartoonist.

If comic books haven't produced the proper antidrug educational attitudes, neither has television. Dr. Paul Lowinger of Wayne State University's School of Medicine, in a statistical survey of television commercials, found "prodrug" messages—those urging the consumption of a drug—outnumbered "antidrug" messages by a ratio of ten to one, "providing impressive support for drug use and abuse in the American public."

Lowinger's rating on the accuracy of these "health messages" was that 30 percent of them were accurate; 57 percent were misleading, 7 percent were inaccurate and misleading.

In what must be one of the major ironies of TV drug education is the viewing of Rod Serling pushing aspirins for a wide variety of ailments and an hour later watching him warn about drug abuse.

According to Senator Gaylord Nelson (D, Wisc.): "The claims made for these non-prescription drugs simply are not supported by scientific evidence." Nelson quotes a few: "'When you need to feel brighter, take Vivarin—it gives you a quick lift' or 'When a sick child brings on simple nervous tension, take Compoz—that little blue pill for simple nervous tension' or 'Leave your feelings of tension behind and slip into the quiet world, You'll feel calmer, more relaxed with Quiet World, the new modern calmative.'"

Nelson and his expert witnesses note that "TV-sponsored mood-altering drugs sold over the counter without prescription are not only ineffective, but also can be quite dangerous. Watching the parents use these emotional crutches has the effect of stimulating children to follow their example. Studies have shown that if the mother is a daily tranquilizer user, then her child is three-and-a-half times as likely to use marijuana, ten times as likely to use opiates such as heroin, five times as likely to use stimulants or LSD and seven times as likely to use tranquilizers."

Nelson noted that "TV drug advertising is fostering a drug culture by promoting the use of drugs advertised to suppress normal emotional reactions to the ordinary frustrations of daily living. As Federal Communications Commissioner Thomas J. Houser has said: 'The television tube is a virtual electronic hypochondriac.' And the drug companies have spent a great deal of money to bring this about—over 300 million dollars in 1970 for drug TV advertising alone. And in all this advertising there is very little worthwhile information given about the product itself. Too often the ads just describe a harried housewife who solves her problem with a pill."

To make matters worse is the fact that "in 1970 three drug companies spent 20 million dollars advertising children's medicines on TV—most of it in sponsoring shows aimed directly at children. Of course many parents rightly resent people pushing pills to children. Federal regulatory agencies such as the Federal Trade Commission and the Federal Communications Commission, which should regulate the TV drug business and protect the public, are in fact protecting the TV drug business, allowing misleading drug advertising—or worse yet, getting the public 'turned on' to drugs by television ads."

New York City Addiction Commissioner Graham S. Finney has denounced the drug industry for its television drug ads promoting a "drugged society." He proposed partial bans or a tax on television drug advertising for addiction rehabilitation programs.

The Federal Trade Commission has recently and unanimously urged the Federal Communications Commission to promulgate regulations mandating "counteradvertising. For example, ads that encourage reliance upon drugs for the resolution of personal problems may be considered by some groups to be a contributing cause to the problem of drug misuse. Counteradvertising would be an appropriate means of providing the public with access to discussion of the issues raised," i.e., a real drug education program.

And if television, comic books, teaching films, and programmed learning do not properly educate people about drug use and abuse, perhaps museums will. According to *Behavior Today*, "The Museum of the City of New York recently focused on the history and treatment of addiction. Guides are all ex-addicts. Also the Smithsonian Institute [*sic*] plans a massive display on drug use to open April 1972. Designed to put drug use in cultural and historical perspective, the exhibit is set for a two-year tour of major cities, following its six-month Washington showing. The 6,000-square-foot exhibit will run well into the six-figure range."

What museums can't educate about addiction, perhaps the U.S. Postal Service can. On October 5, 1971, coinciding with National Drug Abuse Prevention Week (October 3–9) the Postal Service joined in the educational crusade against drug abuse by issuing its first in a series of drug abuse stamps. For eight cents and a self-addressed envelope a first-day cover may be obtained.

But meanwhile, back in the classroom, lectures on heroin have become an expensive fixture of the high school and college curriculums. Even sparsely populated communities have appointed committees charged with promoting drug education.

Drug education classes have something for everyone. Student interest is maintained by allowing them to miss regular class time. Community leaders and bureaucrats get some political mileage by pointing proudly to the number of lectures they have sponsored. Dr. Seymour Halleck says, "Many seem to feel that as long as they keep talking about the heroin problem, it will be solved." Of course, there isn't a shred of evidence to indicate that a single case of addiction has been prevented, retarded, let alone cured, because of, or in spite of, the tens of millions of dollars now being spent on these programs. What does seem clear is that the more money we spend on drug education or addiction educational programs, the faster the addiction rate rises. While there may not be a causative relationship between increasing education and increasing addiction, Halleck, nevertheless, has found that "drug education may even encourage drug addiction." Secondly, ". . . drug education programs may be expensive and ineffective distractions which diminish our motivation to examine basic political questions which may be at the very roots of the heroin problem."

Addiction educational programs flamboyantly attempt to present the horrors of heroin. The theatricality of many of the programs provides a sufficient degree of vicariousness to insure continuing audience interest. Routinely, the program will consist of ". . . one or more meetings at which a local physician, someone from the local police-narcotics unit and a former addict, will endlessly and dramatically catalogue" the grotesqueries of heroin addiction. The physician will exaggerate the degree to which heroin can produce bodily damage, in spite of the fact that heroin, by itself, in an appropriate dosage and purity, produces no bodily damage. The "narc" (narcotics agent) will gravely talk about the increasing flow of heroin into the community and will throw in a few anecdotes about young people he has seen ruined by heroin. Sometimes the narc will even display confiscated glassine envelopes of heroin and the appropriate needles and syringes to horrify the audience. Halleck says, "the former addict, who is usually the star performer, will recount his sordid experiences as a drug user and will glowingly report the salutary effect of his reformation. It is an interesting show which has much the flavor of an old-fashioned revival meeting."

In all likelihood, however, performances by former addicts with a sideshow approach to heroin will probably not have much of a positive influence upon the young people it's aimed at . . . and can possibly have a negative influence. After all, the kids do know better than to accept on a literal basis the evils shown in this kind of presentation. First of all, a sizable proportion of high school and college students have already experimented with drugs such as marijuana and many have found it to be a pleasant experience, rather than a dangerous one. Therefore, when young people hear speakers describe marijuana as a dangerous narcotic, they are understandably skeptical of the speaker's reliability. The students can't help but feel that if the speaker exaggerates about marijuana, he probably exaggerates about heroin.

The National Commission on Marijuana and Drug Abuse has noted that massive miseducation about marijuana has been "remarkable" and has left the public "unsettled." In the age group where most drug education is aimed, the twelve to seventeen age group, the Commission noted that this age group suffered the "most confusion and misconceptions. Many in the group were led to believe that marijuana caused death and was physically addicting. Neither is true."

John Finlator, recently retired deputy director of the Federal Bureau of Narcotics and Dangerous Drugs, says: "We have to deal realistically with the marijuana issue before we can get to the more serious drug issue of heroin. The *rhetoric* and *emotion* surrounding the marijuana debate make significant progress in combatting heroin an impossibility."

Probably the most prominent rationalization offered for the illegalization of marijuana is the belief that marijuana leads to the use of heroin. While this may be true to a limited degree, it seems clear that it is not the marijuana itself, but rather its illegality that forces grass smokers to associate with criminals who are pushing heroin.

Actually it's quite possible that marijuana, rather than leading to heroin, may in fact cut down the number of people switching from marijuana to heroin. For example, in 1970, when the Justice Department's Operation Intercept virtually closed down the Mexican border, in an attempt to suppress marijuana smuggling, it caused a sharp decline in the availability of marijuana to school-age kids.

The heroin traffickers, noting the loss of marijuana, moved into school areas around the country, offering heroin at cut-rate prices in an attempt to create a new market of heroin addicts. They were rather successful, thanks to the removal of its competitor, marijuana.

Among streetwise community leaders it is axiomatic that organized crime is moving into the youth drug scene, not only to take over a potentially profitable marijuana market, but also, by being able to control the flow of marijuana into a community and by stopping that flow at critical times, to turn people on to the far more profitable heroin trade, making permanent and dependent customers of them.

Professor Erich Goode of the State University of New York has called for an end to criminal penalties for the possession of marijuana "thereby cutting the link of illegality between marijuana and heroin, taking the young marijuana user out of the criminal subculture." Legalization of marijuana would end the forced association between criminals and users. Finlator comments on these issues: "In the 1930's, when marijuana was first made illegal, there were less than 50,000 smokers in the whole country. Yet today, after four decades of incredibly harsh penalties, the Marijuana Commission tells us that 50 million Americans have smoked marijuana." Parenthetically, and analogously, according to a *New York Times* study, "America now has more policemen dedicated to the tracking down of drug pushers than in any previous time in its history. But it also has more addicts than in any time in its history." As a result of Finlator's disenchantment with the marijuana laws, he has left the federal government, after thirty-six years, where he was known as "super-narc" because of his hard-nosed tactics in drug law enforcement, to work for the eventual legalization of marijuana. In a semihumorous vein, Columbia University sociologist Amitai Etzioni said that "marijuana cigarettes should not be legalized because they may lead to something far more harmful: tobacco cigarettes."

Dr. Halleck notes that "even the presence of a youthful former heroin addict on the educational program does not have much deterrent effect on the audience. Usually the former addict grew up in an urban ghetto community and his life experiences are unlikely to have been similar to those of most of his audience and thus the audience will have difficulty identifying with him."

As Dr. Tom Levin of Albert Einstein College of Medicine points out, "Most anti-drug programs today are overusing former addicts." Many programs tend to use the former addict as their main educational *and* treatment resource rather than as one part of an overall educational and rehabilitation program. "Furthermore, and even more disturbing, such programs seem to be unaware of a variety of negative consequences of the use of the former addict. For example, the ex-addict may wittingly or unwittingly romanticize drug use and recovery as a passport to special status in the eyes of many youngsters who are dabbling in drugs. The nonaddicted, disadvantaged young person looking for work might be tempted by the advantages of the ex-addict status in seeking jobs in drug abuse programs."

While it is important to point out that many former addicts have a great deal of experience in drug *use* and even in drug *treatment*, they are by definition without personal experience in drug *prevention*. "Not surprisingly, we find that a significant number of ex-addicts, building on personal experience rather than political ideology and training, are much less interested in prevention than in treatment. Much of the abuse and misuse of ex-addicts must

be laid at the door of professionals, particularly those who
have not developed an ideologically rooted, community-
oriented program of their own and who are likely to want
to co-opt the former addict and thus add to the illusion of
in-group special knowledge. Thus a 'conspiracy' is developing among professionals and ex-addicts."

Many drug abuse educational programs fail because
"they have no community programs and no clear political
perspective and because they rely on an alliance of the
presumed experts—the rehabilitated addicts with no experience in drug-abuse prevention and the professionals
isolated from the communities they should serve."

In the classroom setting even a professional ex-addict
has a hard time fooling the kids. The kids read on their
own about heroin, and ask enough of the right questions
to embarrass a speaker who is only familiar with some ex-
aggerated "scare" statistics and experiences. Needless to
say, such an embarrassed speaker is a discredited speaker.
At the same time the speaker's moralistic bases for his
admonitions, rather than his factual bases, are exposed.

Commenting on high-school drug education programs,
federal attorney Whitney Seymour said: "By the time
children have become teenagers, it is almost too late to
affect their thinking about drugs. Last-minute, frantic education efforts for older adolescents are not only a waste of
effort but can have a *boomerang effect.*"

Even when not presenting frantic "scare" material,
Halleck noted, at least in the case of marijuana, that when
". . . I am lecturing groups about the physical and psychological effects of marijuana, and as long as I present only
objective material and do not raise moral questions, the
audience seems to *become progressively more enthusiastic
about the drug*" [emphasis added]. Thus, at least in some
instances, factual approaches to drug education could en-

courage, rather than discourage, experimentation. This is apparently so primarily because the facts de-mystify and "de-terrify" the drug. By the same token, as illegal drugs such as heroin are endlessly discussed and rediscussed, they become more familiar and more acceptable.

Students become even more skeptical about addiction education classes as they come to realize that the use and abuse of legal drugs, particularly those prescribed by physicians, are probably a greater problem for society than the use and abuse of illegal drugs. For example, the National Academy of Science has recently pointed out that roughly 5 percent of all medical hospital admissions are due to reactions secondary to drugs legally obtained and ingested. The Academy also noted that approximately 15 percent of hospital patients go through adverse drug reactions from prescribed drugs. By the nature of these drugs being legal and prescribed, they have become integrated into our way of life and as a result are much more likely to produce more "acceptable" symptoms and consequent problems than heroin. As Dr. Maurice H. Seevers, a member of President Nixon's Commission on Drug Abuse, noted, legal drugs "are a bigger problem because so many more people of all different ages and in all segments of society use them."

For example, the Senate Subcommittee on Juvenile Delinquency reported on December 14, 1971, that certain kinds of barbiturates that can be obtained legally produce an addiction whose withdrawal can be worse than heroin and sometimes fatal. Senator Birch Bayh (D, Ind.) of the Subcommittee said, "Children grow up watching their parents take these pills and they (the children) quickly develop an acceptance of drug taking. Thus casual attitudes toward these potentially destructive drugs, coupled with a legal, readily available supply in the family medicine cabinet, appear intimately connected with the current trend in youthful barbiturate, amphetamine, and ultimately heroin abuse."

In New York State alone 2.6 million people have used amphetamines at least once. The potential numerical dangers of legal amphetamines, Seevers pointed out, was seen "in Japan where large amounts of amphetamines were dumped on the market following the war and an epidemic resulted in which there were up to 2 million *habitual* users producing 55,000 arrests per year." The U.S. National Institute of Health (NIH) estimates that about eight billion legal amphetamine pills are manufactured in the United States each year, or forty amphetamine pills for *each* woman, man, and child in the country.

While the federal government has made some token effort to curb the excessive manufacturing of these pills, the Huntington (N.Y.) Narcotics Guidance Council has chastised the government for allowing seven times the amount of amphetamines needed for legitimate medical purposes to continue to be manufactured.

Because of only token results in curbing amphetamine production, the Federal Bureau of Narcotics and Dangerous Drugs has proposed a quota that will slash amphetamine production by 82 percent. Of course this will only affect licensed U.S. amphetamine manufacturers. It will not affect unlicensed firms, nor foreign firms which arranged for their products to be smuggled into the United States. Nor will the quota affect drugs that are quite similar to, and as dangerous as, amphetamines, namely Ritalin and Preludin—both of which are available by prescription.

All this is to say that making a drug legal or illegal says nothing about its use or abuse, whether by patient, addict, or experimenter. Conventional laws covering drug use and abuse with both legal and illegal drugs border on the irrelevant or worse, as seen in the cases of amphetamines, barbiturates, and heroin.

The Reverend Howard Moody of New York's Judson Memorial Church has hammered away at the "artificiality of many of the drug issues which an amoralistic society and its churches have brought upon themselves by saying certain drugs are bad for people while others are all right, and enforcing these views with punitive laws. I think this is highly immoral."

Seevers notes that heroin has the *reputation* for causing crime in its own right, when in fact it doesn't. Heroin is a depressant, unlike legal amphetamines and other stimulants "which would make one more criminal prone" than heroin. Seevers notes that legal amphetamines and other legal stimulants have caused those who overuse them often to "commit crimes of violence because of damage to brain metabolism." Such cannot be said for heroin.

Prescription drugs, such as amphetamines, barbiturates, and tranquilizers, are massively overused and abused in our society. These drugs do not alleviate specific diseases and have little medical purpose, other than helping people tolerate the stress of everyday life, much the way heroin does. Yet, as Halleck points out, they are prescribed more frequently than any other class of legal drugs and create more problems of addiction and overdosage than does heroin.

Some educators and public officials have suggested that an addiction education program might be improved if athletes, who might exemplify a sound mind in a sound body, and who are often important images to young people, help set good examples by speaking out against drug use.

For example, the white, middle-aged gentlemen who run the powerful National Collegiate Athletic Association

(NCAA) are presently sponsoring a nationwide antidrug educational campaign under the motto, "Get High on Sports, Not Drugs." They have sent teams of muscular athletes and crew-cut coaches around to visit playgrounds, Rotary Clubs, high schools, and colleges all across the country. However, as sports editor Jack Scott points out, "drug abuse is rampant in college athletics and indeed at nearly all levels of athletic competition in our society today." But the NCAA in its antidrug campaign, rather than cleaning their own house, "are spending time and money pushing their slogans and coercing frightened parents into the belief that if they could just get Johnny to cut his hair and turn out for his school's football team, he would be in safe hands."

As Scott shows, nothing could be further from the truth. While coaches have not been maintaining their athletes on heroin, as far as is known, "they have been feeding them anabolic steroids, amphetamines and tranquilizers to the point of abuse." Scott notes that "even an athletic idol like Bill Toomey recently admitted to using drugs to aid his performance in winning the gold medal in the decathlon at the Mexico City Olympics. Toomey, who comes across like Mr. Clean, claims that he swore off drugs before the 1968 Olympics, but then reluctantly returned to them when he arrived in Mexico City intent on winning a gold medal and saw scores of athletes from all over the world popping pills and getting injections." Toomey said it was a dilemma for him: "I didn't take the pills to get ahead of anyone, I took them just to stay even." Other "athletes had their own hypodermic syringes and were giving themselves injections."

Scott goes on to say that the athletes and coaches in Mexico City seldom concerned themselves with debating the morality or medical complications of taking these often dangerous drugs. "In fact, the only debates about drugs that I heard while covering the Olympics were over which drugs were the most effective stimulants and about what kind of amphetamines could go undetected in tests Olympic officials required athletes to take at the conclusion of their competition."

Drug use in the Olympics has skyrocketed to such a degree that the International Olympic Committee on Medical Affairs has ordered a urine sample to be collected from every athlete who finishes within the first six places. The check is to determine if participants have taken stimulants before their events, a forbidden practice. Athletes in the future will be subjected to tests similar to those given race horses.

Scott emphatically says "there is probably no type of highly competitive athletic activity where drugs aren't abused." Tom Ecker, a respected coach, who has authored six books on sports, recently said: "I normally assume that the winner of a sports contest is one who has a better pharmacist than his opponent."

The NCAA may improve their image in Middle America with their "Get High on Sports, Not Drugs" motto, but the truth will be closer to "Get High on Sports With Drugs." Hardly a model for drug-abuse education.

Halleck concludes that the heroin problem is only a symptom of a sickness that pervades our entire, corporately controlled society. Addiction education can be thought of as a treatment that is designed only to treat the symptom, without doing anything about the causes of the illness, and may in fact be contributing to the illness.

Nowadays, even the military has developed its own form of heroin-propaganda education. In spite of the fact that soldiers are usually older than high school students, the military's addiction "education" program attempts to emphasize the same grotesqueries and horrors-of-heroin approach used in the schools—and with about the same degree of success: Congressman Robert Steele estimates that at least 10 percent of all American soldiers in Vietnam have turned to heroin.

Newspaperwoman Gloria Emerson, in a report quoted in the *Congressional Record* in March 1971, said: "In a brigade headquarters at Long Binh, there were reports that heroin use in the unit had risen to 20 percent. You can salute an officer with your right hand and take a 'hit' of heroin in your left. Private Ron McSheffrey added that most of the officers in his company—including the MP's— knew about it."

The heroin peddled to American GIs in Vietnam is easier to get than the morning newspaper. Compared to prices in America, Vietnamese heroin is a bargain, and neither the Saigon government nor the United States Army gets in the way of the heroin trade.

"In many units there are so many GIs using drugs that the only way the commanding officer could stop the problem would be to arrest half the people in his unit. The fact that half the people in his unit were arrested for narcotics would not look good on his record when his turn for promotion came around, so few arrests occur."

In one well-publicized case, Marine Luther Sanford was discharged because he was a heroin addict and sent back to the States. Receiving no treatment before or after discharge, and unable to support his habit in New York City, he managed to reenlist and get sent back to Vietnam, where it was much cheaper and easier to support his habit.

It is so easy to buy heroin from peddlers in Vietnam, wherever there are American troops or convoys, that vials can be purchased outside the headquarters of most American generals. Gloria Emerson noted: "On the 15-mile Bienhoa highway which runs from Saigon north to Long Binh, heroin can be purchased, and was, by this correspondent . . . in a dozen conspicuous places within a few minutes. Many of the salesmen are small children who sit all day underneath a U.S. army poncho pitched like a tarp. They handle quite a bit of money, as well as trade in hard goods, sometimes a carton of cigarettes for a vial of heroin."

As an example of the military's education program for addiction, Forest Kimler, managing editor of the armed forces' *Stars and Stripes* newspaper, described the sort of educational material he likes to see in his paper's anti-heroin program: "I like material that really casts the characters who go for the H (heroin) trip as the real true freaks of society who are destroying themselves. How their bodies are being truly turned into emaciated shells of horror; how their minds are being deranged and twisted into unthinking, craving vacuums of animal lusts and blind desires; how there is no doubt that they are the refuse, the dung on the ash heap of society, the waste that soon will not be able to be reclaimed, with mercifully an unmourned death the only way out for them and for the society that soon will be unwilling and unable to tolerate their continuing existence.

"I don't want the same staid withdrawal-symptoms bit, I want material on subhuman untouchables, committing mass suicide . . . subhumans with the mark of Cain on their forehead and the scarlet letter on their chest . . . subhumans to be institutionalized as they can be dredged from the gutters, but ultimately to be ignored. I want to depict an addict as repulsive, to unleash the Frankenstein monster for what it really is, to brew the horror in the most dramatic fashion. . . ."

As writer Paul Hoffman noted upon reading Kimler's

material, "At a time when the government is supposedly launching a massive rehabilitation effort for those who have become casualties of war through heroin addiction, the last thing those casualties need is to be labeled 'refuse' or 'dung.' " Hoffman wondered what the men in Vietnam would think if they knew that those who direct the war they are fighting consider many of them—as many as one-fifth by some estimates—as "the waste that soon will be unable to be reclaimed, with mercifully an unmourned death the only way out for them."

8 An Army of Addicts

According to the American Civil Liberties Union (ACLU), marijuana used to be plentiful, if not freely available in Vietnam. "But in 1970 it began to disappear from the illicit drug market. In its place pure (95–98 percent) heroin offered by Vietnamese dealers became increasingly available. Unlike marijuana, the small heroin vials are easy to conceal. Heroin is cheap . . . $.80 to $5.00 a vial, less than a can of Coca Cola in many areas of Vietnam. And the white powder can be snorted or smoked without any telltale aroma. An as yet undetermined number of GI users go on to fix the plentiful heroin intravenously."

According to psychoanalyst Dr. Norman E. Zinberg, upon his return from Vietnam: The army itself is universally credited with causing the swing to heroin because of their campaign against marijuana that began around 1968. "Soldiers began using marijuana as far back as 1963; its popularity grew, largely ignored by the Army, until 1968. Then as a result of newspaper stories, the fairly heavy rate of pot smoking, which was evident to everyone, was officially recognized. True to the American tradition, as soon as a problem was identified, a full-fledged

149

assault to stamp it out got under way. Military radio and TV spots proclaimed the evils of marijuana and indicated that a smoker could damage his own brain and become psychotic. 'Drug education' lectures repeating the scare stories about grass became compulsory. In an all-out drive, the Army repeatedly searched billets, sent out officers to sniff for the weed in barracks and secluded fields and even trained marijuana-sensitive dogs.

"It was a very efficient campaign. Marijuana is relatively bulky and the smoke is detectable by smell. In one week there were a thousand arrests for possession of marijuana. Much official satisfaction was expressed in press releases which indicated that 'the' drug problem in Vietnam was being brought under control." Not surprisingly many soldiers simply switched to a stronger, more available, less detectable, cheap drug—heroin.

Newspaper headlines indicate that in 1969 alone there were at least thirty-seven thousand GIs in Vietnam who were strung out on heroin. According to Congressman Robert Steele, in 1969 and 1970, "it is ironic that in these two years of the war our biggest casualty figures came from heroin addiction, not from combat."

Why were so many men in one place using heroin? While the proximity of heroin production in the nearby "fertile triangle" of Southeast Asia is certainly one reason, others are suggested by the soldiers themselves. According to an army psychiatrist, working at a drug rehabilitation center near Longbinh, "Vietnam in many ways is a ghetto for the enlisted man. The soldiers don't want to be here, their living conditions are bad, they are surrounded by privileged classes, namely officers; there is accepted use of violence, and there is promiscuous sex. They react the way they do in a ghetto. They take drugs and try to forget."

Vietnam veteran David Kashimba, in a published ac-

count, wrote: "I served in Vietnam during the TET offensive. This was the time when the heroin problem was
there, but no one knew about it. It was also a time when
the war was just as ridiculous as it is now, but few people
gave it a second thought.

"I could never find anything good in war, but at least
World War II did serve some purpose. The Vietnamese
War has no purpose . . . and the young men in Vietnam are
suffering greatly because of it. No man can live with himself if he feels he has no purpose. This is the originator
of the heroin problem in Vietnam.

"The soldiers often turn to alcohol and marijuana to
create a beautiful world full of happiness and illusions.
When that doesn't work they turn to a harder drug.

"Supporting a war that is for nothing is bad enough,
but when you have to obey with blind obedience leaders
whose lives thrive on war, then your mind starts to de-
teriorate. When you have to kill, not out of self-preserva-
tion, but merely for the sake of your superiors' thirst for
blood, then your mind begins to shatter. Then there are
no other worlds to escape to. Then you must escape your
own mind, and the easiest escape is heroin."

One GI summed it up simply: "Let's face it, I would
never have been on the stuff if they hadn't sent me over
there."

According to Dr. Norman Zinberg, the army's drug
education program operates under the assumption that a
"bad outside force claims an unsuspecting victim. I do not
see it that way. These men are not weak or ignorant. I
think they choose heroin knowingly."

Donald Kirk, in *The New York Times Magazine* article,
"Who Wants To Be the Last American Killed in Vietnam?"
reports that contrary to popular belief about the addict's
passivity and somnolence, the addicts are confronting

their blood-thirsty officers. Kirk visited the once proud
Americal and 101st Airborne Divisions. Kirk, of course,
found no soldier who wanted to be the last American
killed in Vietnam. Kirk did find a widespread use of heroin
with the usual accompaniments—thefts ranging from
stereo sets to food from the mess hall with which to buy
heroin, which in many cases was directly sold by south
Vietnamese soldiers, alongside whom the American soldiers were fighting. The addicts often resorted to "fragging," (derived from fragmentation grenade),—assaults on
overzealous officers who were "gung-ho" to go out on
offensive actions against the Viet Cong. Also numerous
addicts have been found to be involved in blowing up
orderly rooms. Before an actual fragging takes place, the
addict will surreptitiously warn the overzealous officer by
leaving a grenade pin on the officer's pillow. If the officer
doesn't accept the warning, after some indefinite period
of time he stands a good chance of losing a limb or his life.

According to the underground army newspaper *FTA*,
"In some units fraggings now average four a week. Thus
commanders are afraid of what might happen if they attacked the drug users. In 1970, 165,709 GIs went AWOL
and another 65,643 deserted. As a result the populations of
army jails are growing at rates which make it extremely
difficult for the brass to control their prisoners. Many
stockade commanders realize that it is better to overlook a
little drug traffic than it is to have a full-scale riot on their
hands."

A somewhat different view of heroin and "fragging" is
held by Major P.I. Stevenson, an army physician: "When
I first joined the army in Europe, in December 1969, the
army had no dope problem. Of course, there was plenty of
dope being smoked, snorted and shot up, but there was no
dope *problem*, because the army didn't officially recognize
that a problem existed. Everyone laughed and, as usual,

thought the army was stupid. But the army is not stupid; the army is rarely stupid when it comes to protecting its own best interests. Only individuals within the army occasionally fuck up. For in Europe, at least, the army has absolutely nothing to do. Our 'mission,' that is, to hold back the 'eastern hordes' if they launch an aggressive war and cross the border, is not taken seriously by *anyone*. The most naive farm kid who spends two years walking up and down the border does not really believe that he is going to hold back the Communist hordes once the 'balloon goes up' . . . a favorite army expression here referring to the hydrogen bomb. Even the official propagandists on army radio have tired of stating how important our 'mission' is to the safety of freedom and democracy.

"And nothing to do breeds boredom and lack of morale. According to David Bender of *The New York Times*, 'for a regiment or a division, whose principal mission is to guard a section of the Soviet bloc border, the major enemy seems to be boredom. The problem comes up at every level. The most extreme of which is, the drug abuse among young draftees.'

"Even in Vietnam there is more morale than in Germany, which might prove the old point, that even a crummy 'enemy' is better than a phantom enemy. And boredom and lack of morale, compounded with shitty housing and a universal feeling of alienation in Europe, especially among the blacks (in Vietnam even the blacks had the 'chinks' and the 'gooks' to shit on) and pre-existing racial tensions present a powder keg that the army is quite well aware of. The phony field exercises where men must 'play war' do not help much. It is *dope*, more than anything else, that keeps the powder keg from exploding more often than it has. (We've already had plenty of bad 'race riots.')

"A large portion of GIs go around stoned all day. The

saying here is: 'If you're not stoned on dope, you're out on juice.' Snorting and shooting heroin occur right under the noses of sergeants and commanders. Yet their attitude has always been: 'If they can do the job, it's all right with me.' Translated: 'I'd rather have them out and inefficient than aware and dangerous.' In effect heroin and other drugs become the army's own internal counterinsurgency and pacification device.

"Now everything has been complicated by the army's having been forced to recognize officially that it has a 'problem.' The army says, of course, that narcotics are not their problem, but that the GIs just brought their 'pre-existing' problems in with them; that the army's dope problem is a reflection of society's dope problem. In a sense they have a point. In any event, commanders have been relieved of their command over their failure to make a *show* of doing something about the problem; so everyone must have a narcotics program. We have, therefore, an unbelievable network of paper programs and white-wash. Regardless, the use of dope continues to be encouraged, almost *forced* by the system. Few GIs, and these are usually very bright or very politically aware, resist the use of anything.

"In Vietnam, the problem takes on different twists. A vial of heroin on the streets of Saigon contains 250 milligrams and is 95 percent pure. The vial costs a little over $2.00 in U.S. money. The same net amount of heroin on the streets of New York costs about $300.00. At first it was widely speculated upon by the army that the Viet Cong or North Vietnamese 'psyops' (psychological operations) divisions had infiltrated their 'dirty' dope on our clean American fighting men to destroy their fighting spirit. It seemed inconceivable that there was a profit motive in selling anything so cheaply when a higher price could easily have been asked. (It's important to remember that prices of goods in the inflated economy of Vietnam are actually quite high, especially for those things that soldiers want, such as prostitutes.) Then it began to be discovered that the pure heroin was being carried by the CIA's Air America transport planes in Vietnam. And the people involved in the distribution were south Vietnamese officials working along with American officials.

"Heroin is so plentiful and accessible in Vietnam that according to Dr. Norman E. Zinberg, 'anyone who *doesn't* want to take the drug must be the one to say so. And the GI doesn't creep off alone to a sleazy pad or doorway to nod after a hit. Heroin consumption in Vietnam is a *social* activity among *groups* of friends.'

"All this has been known for years by the army, at least according to people here who were in Vietnam working with drug addicts years ago. Yet, only a couple of people and now American upper-echelon officers have just recently been implicated. Was there such a great profit in the local drug trade? Regardless, why has the army continued to tolerate known distribution channels right within its own midst, at the same time, ironically enough, talking about the drug problem, its treatment centers, etc.? I doubt, therefore, that one can implicate only an immediate profit motive.

"A stoned soldier who agrees to walk ('point' as leader) down a mined road is preferable to an undrugged soldier who will do no such irrational thing. A stoned soldier firing at the 'enemy' is still better than an undrugged soldier firing at his own superiors."

According to a UPI report of January 24, 1972, in an attempt to keep peace within the increasingly disgruntled ranks of Americans in Vietnam, "the Army has opened its gates to Vietnamese prostitutes at several bases in south

Vietnam. An Army spokesman said such a thing is permissible under current regulations. Officers, however, note that there were many security risks and a strong possibility of narcotics smuggling."

Former Vice-President Ky himself early stated that he would open brothels for American troops. Ky had built a brothel-massage-drug complex exclusively for the American soldiers at An Khe. Charles Winick describes a GI's visit to the complex at An Khe: "Before I could enter the main area I had to pick up a rubber and pass an exam on how to use it. Then I got a great haircut, manicure, some great dope, and a blow job. When I left the complex the MP at the gate told me to wash myself to avoid clap."

One of President Nixon's responses to the army's heroin problem is to push his "Drug Abuse Counter-Offensive," the so-called heroin "amnesty program." According to Samuel A. Simon, now serving as a captain in the Judge Advocate General's Corps, U.S. Army, the program is designed to encourage heroin addicts to turn themselves in for treatment. The essence of the program is to assure military addicts that they will not be prosecuted if they voluntarily seek help. The program, announced with much fanfare and great expectations, has never really gotten off the ground.

At first, Simon notes, resistant commanders made every effort to thwart full implementation of drug amnesty. For example, at one base the commander instructed the Criminal Investigation Division (army detectives) to institute an investigation into drug use so broad in scope that it involved most of the enlisted soldiers under his command. Since a prerequisite to receiving amnesty is that one must not have been under investigation by the military police, this action nullified the program at the base.

As the program has slowly gained some command support, however, a more basic problem has appeared: even when fully applied, the program offers only a limited form of amnesty. In fact, substantial adverse consequences, both during and after service, still await the heroin addicts who turn themselves in for treatment. Yet the soldier is indoctrinated from the day he enters the military with the virtues and protection of the drug amnesty program. Everyone from the soldier's company commander to the President of the United States has assured him that if he turns himself in as an addict no punitive action will be taken. Deputy Assistant Secretary of the Army John Kester stated at the National Heroin Symposium in July 1971: "I can assure you, a serviceman's addiction will not show up in any permanent records."

However, according to a recent report from the American Civil Liberties Union: "Despite the fact that anonymity was originally promised to participants in the program (i.e., there were to be no permanent records identifying drug abusers), the promise was often broken and recently it was officially rescinded. Identification as a drug abuser is now part of the individual's permanent military record." Many of the soldiers who believed they were volunteering for anonymity in the amnesty program found themselves ill prepared for the hostility that greeted them on return to their units, once they were identified as drug users. "They were assigned to menial and demeaning tasks and confronted with derogatory attitudes and harassment from superiors." Because of these "flaws" (and others) in the "amnesty" program, "only a small fraction of drug abusers have sought treatment."

Specifically a March 1972 Pentagon report published by United Press International said that the Pentagon "stamps the number SPN384 on the records of servicemen discharged for using drugs, permanently identifying them as drug abusers to prospective employers and supervisors." Because this stamping procedure is used indiscriminately on both full-fledged addicts, as well as those who simply may have experimented with heroin, or simply had a "false positive" in the urine testing program, Senator Harold Hughes promised legislative action to stop the practice because "it brands men for life for indiscretions committed while they were young, often with a supply of drugs literally pushed on them."

Dr. Richard S. Wilbur, assistant secretary of Defense for Medical Affairs and close relative of Dr. Dwight Wilbur, past president of the American Medical Association, called Hughes' attempt at stopping this publicizing of addicts "too bad, because it is valuable for an employer to know about a man's problems." Hughes noted that a man so identified would be unlikely to wind up with an employer.

A GI paper, *Forward*, supporting Senator Hughes, noted in an article entitled "Welcome Home!": "Businessmen, who once cheered on 'our boys' in Vietnam, despise returned veterans. Take for example the New York State Chamber of Commerce which recently published a pamphlet, 'Drug Abuse as a Business Problem,' advising members not to hire vets. The pamphlet says, 'With the spread of drug abuse in schools and particularly among members of the armed forces in Vietnam, it would be unrealistic for business to assume it could recruit from these markets and not risk bringing drug abuse, narcotics addicts and pushers into companies, despite all sophisticated screening available.' Some prospective employers turn down Vietnam vets because these employers believe them *all* to be heroin addicts."

Hughes said to Wilbur: "Have you no knowledge of what this identification does to a man for the rest of his days. When does a man ever get rid of this number, SPN384?" Hughes added that "discharges from the armed services for drug abuse rose by nearly 40 percent from 1970 to 1971 alone. Are men being turned out of the service after only a cursory attempt to treat them?"

A *New York Times* investigation into this issue of cursory treatment revealed that "The U.S. Army is discharging large numbers of heroin users despite pledges from President Nixon and the Pentagon to keep drug addicts in the Army for special help and rehabilitation. Between 1,000 and 3,000 GIs are being discharged each month, according to an official source, after having been *twice* certified as heroin users. Army officials note that it is unlikely that these men have *even started* to be cared for or treated by the time they leave, in spite of the fact of President Nixon's announcement that the 'military services would retain for treatment *any* [emphasis added] individual due for discharge who is a narcotics addict—*all* [emphasis added] our servicemen must be accorded the right to rehabilitation.'"

As Senator Harold Hughes points out, "cursory treatment, discharge and little rehabilitation is obviously no solution. On the contrary, it fatally compounds the problem. These men are trained in *violence* and guerrilla warfare and are being returned home afflicted with a deadly crime-inducing disease they can't control. Vietnam veteran and addict Francisco Rivera told reporters that he 'relied on my escape and evasion training and pulled off fifty successful burglaries in the Bronx.'"

Vietnam veteran and addict Richie Linder says it was "the reconnaissence training that saved me from the junkies' scramble. After ten months with a Special Forces intelligence unit in Vietnam, my specialty now is banks and apartments of pushers." Incidentally, Rivera received a Silver Star, three Bronze Stars, and four Purple Hearts; Linder received a Silver Star, a Bronze Star, and a Purple

Heart. In the States, where the cost of illegal heroin and other narcotics is high, the only way that most addicts can support their habit is by crime.

Similarly, President Nixon was reported by the *Washington Post* of July 18, 1971, to have assured soldiers that punitive action would not be taken against those who volunteer for treatment. Nevertheless, more and more soldiers are finding that in actuality "amnesty" doesn't mean amnesty.

First, amnesty applies only to the "crime" of possession and use of drugs. It does not apply to possession of large amounts of drugs, to selling drugs, or to drug-related offenses. If in the course of granting amnesty or during subsequent treatment it is discovered that the soldier committed some other crime, he will be tried for that offense. Thus the heroin addict who returns from Vietnam and finds that he must steal to support his habit in the United States—and virtually all addicted GIs must steal to support their habits—and then turns himself in will be subject to court-martial for theft. Moreover, the probability of related offenses coming to light is fairly high, since in the military there is no such thing as a privileged communication between doctor and patient.

Second, whenever a soldier enters the drug amnesty program he *automatically* cuts off all veteran and disability benefits for treatment of drug-related injury or disease which he might otherwise be entitled to after leaving the service. In addition, he will be required to add the time spent in treatment to the length of his tour of duty. These results stem from the military system of assigning blame for every injury or disease incurred by a soldier while on active duty. If an injury or disease is considered to have been incurred "not in the line of duty" and "due to the soldier's own misconduct," the soldier will be required by law to make up the time spent in treating the injury or disease and will be denied veterans' benefits related to the injury or disease. "Line of duty" is a vague term, and unless a soldier intentionally inflicts harm upon himself or is grossly negligent, injuries are normally so classified. However, the exception to this is an army regulation which states that any injury or disease directly resulting from "intemperate" use of drugs will be considered to have been incurred "not in the line of duty," but rather "due to one's own misconduct."

Although it would seem simple enough to adopt a restrictive definition of "intemperate" and hold that in the future all but cases of obvious overdoses of drugs will be considered to have been incurred in the line of duty, this has not been done.

Third, a soldier who enters the drug amnesty program runs the risk that this fact will be used as evidence against him in subsequent administrative or court-martial proceedings. It is possible, for example, that a soldier will be granted amnesty for drug use or possession, be tried for a theft committed to support the habit, and at the court-martial on the theft offense have the fact of drug use or addiction presented as evidence both on the merits and in the portion of the trial on sentencing.

In addition, drug use or addiction will be a major factor in administrative proceedings used to eliminate addicts from the service. If the administrative elimination is based *solely* on addiction, the regulations now require that an honorable discharge be given. But frequently a soldier who has submitted to treatment under amnesty will be subject to elimination for other reasons. In these proceedings, addiction will be a significant factor considered by the soldier's superior officers when making their recommendations as to retention and type of discharge to be given.

Oddly enough, the same situation does not exist under

the urine sample program, described below. The regulation implementing the urine sample requirement in the United States for all soldiers going to Vietnam or leaving the army specifically states that any information received as the result of the obligatory urine sample, or in the treatment of addicts thus discovered, cannot be used in any other proceedings against the addict-soldier. At first sight the military would seem to have made an effort to avoid the anomalies of the drug amnesty program. At least with respect to court-martial proceedings, the regulation does nothing more than provide what the law already requires. It is clear that the urine sample is taken as the result of an illegal general search not based on probable cause and could not be competent evidence in any court. In fact, there is some doubt about the legality of the urine sample requirement itself, on the ground that it constitutes an illegal invasion of privacy contrary to the Fourth Amendment.

A number of other adverse consequences threaten the soldier who submits to treatment under drug amnesty, among them loss of security clearances and job transfers. Yet many soldiers would no doubt want to enter the program even with full knowledge of all the dangers. The problem is that the average soldier is rarely fully informed and relies instead on false assurances from the president and members of the military establishment.

The result is that most soldiers do not become aware of the hazards of participating until they have gone beyond the point of no return. Once he asks for amnesty, a soldier finds that he must accept all that goes with it—loss of benefits, extension of his tour of duty, loss of security clearance, etc.,—or withdraw from amnesty and be prosecuted on the heroin use offense. In short, all that the military has been able to do, with apparent great effort, is develop "amnesty with a catch."

A Senate subcommittee on drug abuse in the military reported on January 28, 1972, that "the average service-man fears the armed services amnesty program for drug users. He is convinced that it is laced with punitive booby traps and that it will force him to squeal on his buddies. The suspicion of the men would appear to have grounds."

The subcommittee said: "At the present time the program does not appear to be working with any marked success as is witnessed by the small percentage of men participating in it."

With the "amnesty program" failing, another aspect of Nixon's heroin program is first to identify the addicts and then to get them on methadone, forcefully, if necessary. Before leaving Vietnam all military personnel are *required* to take a urinalysis test, which detects small quantities of opiates, i.e., heroin derivatives. To insure the validity and reliability of the testing procedure, each man is kept under surveillance through a one-way mirror while he ". . . urinates on command," and is commonly known as "Operation Golden Flow." Sophisticated GIs, however, have learned that salt added to the urine sample invalidates the test. Others invalidate the test by going off heroin four to five days prior to testing.

Regardless of whether or not urine testing can be invalidated by sophisticated GIs or other addicts, many questions about the ethics of such testing are being raised. Professor Thomas Szasz, physician and psychiatrist, complains that:

"Those who have joined the war against illegitimate drug taking never tire of telling us about the terrible things illegal drugs do to the brain or the liver, the kidney or the germ plasm. There is, however, another kind of harm that, though less dramatic than death from an overdose of heroin, is in many ways more far-reaching and devastating: the destruction of the moral integrity of the medical profession. By turning doctors into detectives, whose zealous pursuit of the 'drug abuser' brooks no opposition, the war against drug addiction has blunted the ethical sensibilities of physicians.

"The urines of all servicemen returning from Vietnam are now tested for evidence of 'drug abuse.' The medical profession has accepted this testing, whether the servicemen like it or not, as a perfectly reasonable precaution against the spread of the 'drug epidemic' to mainland America. But from the standpoint of medical ethics, such testing is not as simple as it seems. For if testing the urine of soldiers for heroin is good for the country, perhaps testing the blood of legislators for alcohol, especially when they are drafting important bills or voting on them, would be even better for it. My point is not to propose the medical control of legislators, but to protest the medical control of servicemen. (I am opposed to any such compulsory medical interventions.)

"The crusade against 'drug abuse' operates on the premise that the end justifies the means. One of the methods that has thus become as acceptable in the struggle against 'drug abuse' as the chest film has in the struggle against tuberculosis is deliberate, conscious mendacity. Here is an illustration from a recent article by A.G. Blumberg and others entitled 'Covert Drug Abuse Among Voluntary Hospitalized Psychiatric Patients' appearing in a 1971 issue of the *Journal of the American Medical Association*. The article reported that 'the urine analytic data were kept completely secret from all other members of the staff, and at no time were the patients or staff aware that the urine samples were being monitored for abusable drugs. . . .

Under the guise of a statistical survey of urinary creatinine, urine samples were collected every Monday morning, since it was thought that the highest incidence of drug abuse would take place over the weekends.' To carry out their study, the authors evidently believed that it was perfectly reasonable and morally proper to lie about what they were doing. Furthermore the editors of the official journal of the American Medical Association who read and accepted this study for publication must also have approved, for they featured the report as a lead article.

"The authors claim that they have published a report on 'covert drug abuse.' I submit they have inadvertently published a report on the 'covert abuse of medicine': narrowly, on the abuse of testing urine, and broadly, on the abuse of the trust patients place in their physicians.

"It matters not for what interest the physician sacrifices the sacred heritage of his patients' trust: for money, like the greedy under capitalism; or for medicine itself, like the true believers in 'therapeutic salvation' everywhere. In each case the result is the same: the loss by the physician of his patients' trust; and the progressive transformation of the medical relation from compassion and cooperation in the interest of treating the patient, to deception and coercion in the interest of controlling him."

In an attempt to "re-validate" the testing procedures, the military's urine samples are no longer collected only at the two major debarkation points of Cam Rahn Bay and Long Binh. Urine samples are now collected in "sweeps" of various rear areas, as well, where automated facilities theoretically screen all departing or nearly departing troops for heroin. However, these automated testing mechanisms, e.g., the Free Radical Assay Technique (FRAT), Gas Liquid Chromatography (GLC), and Thin Layer Chromatography (TLC) all produce, with a great degree of regularity, both false positives and false negatives. The American Civil Liberties Union (ACLU) notes that a number of individuals receive positive urines for smoking marijuana or taking cough syrup that might contain trace amounts of opium and as a result are channeled into the program along with the regular addicts.

As reported by Jon Stewart, a San Francisco journalist just back from Vietnam, "Officers are required to oversee the administration of the urine and other tests and are thereby able to avoid taking them themselves." Therefore, at virtually all rehabilitation centers there are no patients above the rank of staff sergeant, even though hundreds of officers are known to be addicted.

Once a positive result is obtained, the ACLU states that "the GI is separated from his departing unit and placed in either the Sixth Convalescent Center (6th CC, Company A) at Cam Rahn Bay or 'T.C. Hill' (6th CC, Company B) in Long Binh. Rights of an appeal to a physician are given to all who show positive opiate identification. But according to returning veterans, such appeals are likely to be successful only if the man is an officer, and unsuccessful for the average soldier, particularly if he is black or considered 'radical' by Army standards."

In one well-publicized case of a soldier being falsely positively identified for heroin use, Sergeant Donald L. Fryer told a Senate subcommittee that he was put into a "detoxification unit in Vietnam and held behind barbed wire for 10 days after an Army urinalysis machine mistakenly identified him as a drug user." Fryer said his protestations of innocence got no sympathy from the physician in charge, who insisted that "the machine must be right" and accused him of being "uncooperative," in spite of the fact that Freyer "had been awarded six battle stars, a Bronze star with cluster and a Good Conduct ribbon and an Army Commendation medal for his work against drug abuse." It required only ten days for Freyer to be "cleared" of drug abuse. What happens to those with fewer military credentials?

If a soldier chooses to enter a rehabilitation program, according to Stewart, "he's put in a five day lock-up and is shot up with methadone." Often soldiers who had only traces of heroin in their urine, who have only experimented with heroin, but have not become addicted, have become addicted to the government's addicting methadone.

While the rehabilitation program is nominally a matter of individual choice, those who did not wish to become "rehabilitated" have had the option of accepting an Undesirable Discharge, which effectively eliminates their chance of holding most jobs in the United States. However, even the nominally voluntary aspects of this program were discarded when President Nixon's narcotic aide, Dr. Jerome Jaffe, announced that ". . . addicted servicemen will be tested and treated against their will" (*The New York Times*, September 19, 1971), thus increasing the number of GIs who will become addicted to the government's methadone.

Congressman John Murphy (D, N.Y.) noted on September 20, 1971, that GI drug treatment facilities at home and abroad ". . . range from the farcical to the inept." In a report to the House Commerce Committee, Murphy added that "I have found many of them to be without form, content, or the necessary expertise to achieve any sort of acceptable results. These programs were hastily conceived, or conceived in desperation; put into operation piecemeal and predictably executed in either a disorganized or pedantic fashion. . . . While we have not reached the point where drug use has severely hampered the overall ability of the military to carry out its mission, i.e., the defense of the United States, if proper steps are not taken, we will eventually reach that stage based on current trends. . . . In all of the programs there is a dislike, distrust and disenchantment on the part of the patients for the treatment received."

For example, at the two major treatment centers in Vietnam, at the Long Binh and Cam Ranh Bay 6th Convalescent Centers (6th CC), the ACLU notes:

"Returnees from the two centers report that conditions are basically prison-like and complain of being treated like 'animals' and 'criminals.' On admission, 'patients' are relieved of all personal property and valuables, stripped and body searched, including digital rectal examinations, and assigned to a ward. At the 6th CC, there is an intensive care unit for those with severe drug withdrawal symptoms or other serious complaints, a regular barracks area and a maximum security area for so-called recalcitrant patients. The compound is surrounded by barbed wire and guarded by armed MPs. An atmosphere of fear and hostility is pervasive, and patients are often harassed and referred to as 'junkies' and 'dope fiends.' Many complain of mistreatment or no treatment at all. Others tell of frequent shakedown inspections without warning or explanation. Conditions were such that in the fall of 1971, a major riot occurred in which two barracks were set ablaze.

"In the 6th CC, as elsewhere in Vietnam, Conex boxes and other small wooden enclosures are sometimes used for confinement and punishment. The boxes, designed for storing supplies, are about six feet high (a tall man can't stand), five feet wide and eight feet long. Holes are cut out for ventilations, locks and bars placed on doors, and sometimes partitions placed inside so that two people may be confined in one box.

"Reasons for confinement to a Conex or maximum security ward vary from major offenses such as striking a guard or trying to escape, to such minor offenses as being unable to urinate when samples are collected, being verbally abusive, staying in the bathroom past 10 P.M., or refusing a work detail, sometimes because of severe withdrawal symptoms.

"The Conexes are very hot in summer and likewise cold in winter, have no sanitary facilities, and depending on who is on guard duty, 'prisoners' frequently are forced to use tin cans because their guard won't permit them to go out to a latrine. Patients often go through heroin withdrawal while in a Conex without benefit of any medication.

"At Long Binh Jail, rows of Conex containers form the maximum security part of the stockade. This area is known to former occupants as 'Silver City' and part of Long Binh Jail is now reportedly being converted into a Drug Abuse Holding Company. Prisoners of Long Binh stockade who are confined to Conex boxes report that vermin abound and that rat bites are not uncommon.

"Two negative urine samples are required before a patient can be evacuated to one of 33 designated rehabilitation facilities on military posts in the United States. What little 'treatment' exists consists primarily of throwing drug users together with other drug users, most of whom are essentially not motivated to give up heroin. The 'therapeutic' aspect of these programs emphasizes how and why the soldier got into drug use. 'The drug' becomes an inescapable topic. On purely logical grounds, a program should at least attempt to get the patient away from this preoccupation with the drug. More importantly is whether those in the involuntary treatment centers, men brought together against their will who share a bitterness towards the Army, will manage to maintain their ties with one another in civilian life. As Dr. Norman Zinberg points out, 'It is possible that the strong group feelings at these centers might prepare the ground for a *social network* that could make heroin *easier to obtain in the U.S.*' "

The "patients" may be kept in Vietnam after their normal Vietnam release date (though—as yet—not after their service release date). "For the trip home, some are strapped down in litters and given tranquilizers (often despite vigorous objections)."

The ACLU notes: "In addition to identification and initial 'rehabilitation' of drug abusers, attention is now being focused on the possibility of long term follow-up into civilian life. The form of follow-up being contemplated is not yet clear. Apparently the program would involve surveillance.

"In an interview with *Army Times* (Oct. 20, 1971), Dr. Jerome Jaffe, director of the Drug Abuse Counter-Offensive, admitted that 'certain groups' would protest the action as an 'invasion of privacy.'

"In addition to the military aspects of surveillance of addicts, Jaffe has come out strongly for 'testing in schools and other institutions. The trail for this was blazed by Central State University at Wilburforce, Ohio, where urinalysis for opiates was made a requirement for quarterly registration.' In defending his position, Jaffe said, '. . . this action is nothing more than *normal* [emphasis added] medical technique employed regularly in the scientific and academic community.' Also, under Jaffe's plan, soldiers diagnosed as drug dependent would be involuntarily held beyond the time of their service obligation to undergo treatment at Veterans Administration Centers.

"Despite the crackdown, the use of hard drugs in Vietnam is widely acknowledged to be in excess of the 5 percent currently being identified by mass urine screening.

The President's counteroffensive is not having its intended effect. It is having another effect: Many GIs returning to the United States are distrustful of all rehabilitative treatment. They are antagonized by the generally unsympathetic attitudes concerning the problems which led to their use of hard drugs, and by the systematic transgression of their civil liberties—their protection against self-incrimination, illegal search and seizure, cruel and unusual punishment, and arbitrary punitive procedures. The medical problem is not being solved by the drug counteroffensive, but a formidable legal problem is being created."

As one reads through this book one may become increasingly aware of the competition and contradictions within, between, and among various agencies as they often *both* prosecute and protect the heroin trade. For example, in the above situation military police prosecute and persecute GI heroin users. In other situations Military Intelligence works with the CIA in heroin transportation. In still another situation the January 24, 1971, wire services reported that, "Conflicts between two Federal agencies have reached the point where officials of the Customs Bureau have arrested agents of the Bureau of Narcotic and Dangerous Drugs." One can only guess that the various federal, state, and local agencies are in fact under considerable pressure to do both, prosecute and protect the heroin empire.

In spite of the fact that in June of 1971 President Nixon declared illicit drugs the "Number One" enemy, Congressman Don Edwards, (D, Cal.) said a report by the General Accounting Office shows ". . . heroin addicts are being turned away by the busload at Public Health Hospitals, although these hospitals are operating at just half of capacity." Parenthetically, Edwards also said a program enacted by Congress to give drug addicts arrested on fed-

eral crimes a choice of being rehabilitated instead of imprisoned, has barely been used by the Justice Department.
Edwards said the government's own report "documents
the abysmal inadequacies of federal drug rehabilitation
efforts."

The problems of heroin addiction are not only a problem
for the United States military in Southeast Asia, but are
increasingly a problem for the Veterans' Administration
(VA) in the United States. As reported by Associated
Press reporter Jean Heller, heroin addiction in discharged
GIs from Vietnam has led to rampant drug dealing in VA
hospitals. While VA headquarters in Washington attempts
to minimize the problem, numerous local VA hospital
directors are "scared stiff," noting that heroin addiction
and dealing is *the* major source of violent crime *inside*
their hospitals and that it is nearly impossible to stop it.

The problems of being a soldier in Vietnam do not stop
once the soldier leaves Vietnam. Numerous VA physicians
point to what they consider a major factor in a veteran's
continued use of heroin, PVS, the Post-Vietnam Syn-
drome. While it is hardly a clear diagnostic category, PVS
is rather a malaise that embraces intangibles undetected in
past military conflicts: moral corruption, alienation, guilt;
having been compelled to be both "victim and execu-
tioner"; having been made to serve in a class and race war
for no discernible reason, by a nation that cared little for
them; being held morally responsible in an amoral whirl-
wind. This war is a cruel hoax, an American tragedy, literally leaving large numbers of young Americans holding
the bag.

Dr. Otto Shaefer, director of the VA psychiatric facility
at Coatsville, Pennsylvania, says, "Our internal crime
problem, secondarily to heroin traffic, is definitely increasing. We've had a rush of thefts and holdups *within* the

hospital. The younger patients have been holding up the helpless geriatric patients for money to buy their heroin. Just last night two young patients here robbed an older patient. They stole his wallet and then threw the covers up over the old man's head so his screams couldn't be heard. We've also had a series of thefts in the hospital staff housing quarters and muggings outside on the hospitable grounds. Most of the time it's impossible to catch the culprits. At night we just don't have enough guards to stop it." One VA official who asked to remain anonymous noted that "theft and violence, as a part of the heroin trade, has become so common in VA hospitals that it's coming to be part of the treatment program."

In an attempt to stop the heroin traffic, one VA chief physician stated that "We have periodic, unannounced searches and often turn up heroin. It's not uncommon for a patient to come here from another ward and say he's been shooting up every day for four months before anybody discovered it. It's not something you can easily put a stop to. This is a 694-bed hospital and there are hundreds of people in and out of the building every day. Short of a thorough search of each patient and visitor every day, there's no way to keep heroin out. It's easier to carry and hide than a bottle of liquor."

While no one in the VA system has been able to estimate the number of their patients involved in addiction problems or heroin traffic or even in which hospitals they're concentrated, Michael Burns, executive director of Paralyzed Veterans of America, charged before a U.S. Senate subcommittee that heroin use was particularly widespread in spinal-cord-injury wards. "If the VA were ever to open the Pandora's box on heroin use in those wards," he said, "it would make any other study on heroin seem like nothing."

The director of the Atlanta VA hospital first learned about the drug traffic in his hospital when nurses reported that they had gone to a patient's room to prepare him for surgery and ". . . found that he already had 'premedicated' himself."

In other circumstances VA hospitals have been raided by federal, state, and local police, where both patients and staff have been arrested because of their active involvement in the hospital's heroin traffic.

And the returning addicted veterans are bringing home with them more than just heroin. A public health official, who requested anonymity, stated that recent epidemics in the United States indicate that malaria seems to be returning from the jungles of Indochina via young American veterans' blood and is being pumped into civilians by the sharing of needles and syringes among addicts. Dirty injection equipment can pass malaria as well as hepatitis and other infectious diseases of the blood.

Mosquito-spread malaria disappeared from the United States after World War II. However, with the return of our servicemen from Vietnam, malaria is being imported almost as commonly as VD.

"Shooting up" malaria is reaching epidemic proportions among addicts. Since July 1970 at least four separate outbreaks have occurred—two of them in California, with one involving over fifty people.

The malaria parasite is transferred in infected red blood cells when a person with the disease contaminates his syringe and/or needle equipment with his own blood and then shares that equipment with another person. Passing even one infected, microscopic-size cell may be enough to spread the infection. The incubation period—the time from acquisition of infection to the onset of symptoms—may be from several days to three weeks.

Fortunately, most of the malaria spread among drug users so far has been the nonfatal variety. However, the serious, fatal kind frequently is imported from Vietnam, and it can be spread as easily as the less serious variety.

The fourth geopolitical reason for a continuing heavy concentration of heroin development in Indochina is the potentially rich market of American officials and their dependents now living in the area, if not outrightly controlling it. Thomas Marlowe of the Pacific News Service reported that in the Spring of 1971 two American teen-age dependents of U.S.A.I.D. program employees were caught mailing twenty kilograms of pure heroin through the APO (U.S. military and governmental postal service) in Vientiane, Laos. The drugs were addressed for Saigon, where they were to be picked up by other A.I.D. dependents, who were then to use or sell the drug.

As a result of this exposure no one under eighteen years of age is now allowed to mail anything larger than a letter through the Vientiane APO.

Several days after the boys were caught, the son of a well-placed embassy official admitted confidentially that "I was all ready to mail ten pounds of heroin to the States. I had it all packed and a buyer waiting at the other end, but now it is too risky. The APO is checking every package going out."

Heroin is thus not only deeply entrenched in the American military forces, but it also reaches the entire American diplomatic community in Southeast Asia. Among those who will return to the United States with a heroin habit are a number of American teen-age dependents of U.S. Embassy, AID, CIA, as well as military officials. Many of these dependents live at K-M6, a compound outside Vientiane for American officials and their families. At the K-M6 high school, one ninth-grader was reported by Marlowe as saying, "Almost everyone past the sixth grade smokes grass here. A lot of the older kids are using heroin."

But the American dependents in Laos are not the only ones hit by the spreading heroin problem. In Thailand, at least one American student at the Bangkok International School died from an overdose of heroin last year and fourteen others were expelled for heroin usage. Marlowe reports he was told that ". . . those were only the constant violators, you know, the kids who go into the bathroom and shoot up between classes." Scores of others are more discreet and don't get caught.

The psychiatric ward at Bangkok's 5th Field Hospital has grown accustomed to American dependents on heroin. A psychiatric ward medic told Marlowe, "There's always a 13- or 14-year-old kid in there for smack [heroin]." A hospital psychologist there mentioned that "It hurts worst when a twelve- or thirteen-year-old girl is brought in with a heroin overdose. I've seen little girls with needle marks on their arms. Their parents often cry and want to know why. The kids say that they just wished someone cared."

To support their habits or just to make money, some of the kids, like those caught mailing the heroin, sell the drug. Unlike GIs, who generally have an intense dislike for "heavy pushers," some of the teen-age "heavy pushers" in Southeast Asia feel that "somebody will do it, why not me?" The reason "why it shouldn't be me" is that the heroin trade in Southeast Asia is as vicious as it is on the streets of Harlem or Watts. For example, shortly after Christmas of 1970, the seventeen-year-old son of a U.S. AID official was shot and killed in a Bangkok alleyway. "He had not," according to one of his former associates, "paid his Thai supplier the full amount for the last shipment of heroin he received."

In an effort to prevent heroin from reaching families of United States officials (as opposed to the military) stationed in Southeast Asia, the Dispatch News Service reports that "one of the main problems of the U.S. antidrug effort is that it involves, in many instances, reversing long-standing U.S. policies of using the local drug traffic to cement local anti-communist alliances. In Thailand, for example, where antidrug activities are at best described as 'lethargic' and where American-backed officials have long been involved in the opium trade, American agents have recently been authorized to use 'extra legal' methods—including assassination—to eliminate traffickers who refuse to be wooed out of business by compensating U.S. construction contracts." As one United States official commented, "You don't do it all with law enforcement."

As investigative journalists Frank Browning and Banning Garrett said of the "new opium war," "The U.S. went on a holy war to stamp out communism and to protect its Asian markets, and it brought home heroin. It is a fitting trade-off, one that characterizes the moral quality of the U.S. involvement in Southeast Asia . . . Heroin has now become the newest affliction of affluent America—of mothers who only wanted to die when they traced track-marks on their daughters' often elegant arms, or of fathers, speechless in outrage when their conscripted sons came back from the war bringing, as their only lasting souvenir, a blood-stained needle."

As the use of heroin in Vietnam and elsewhere increases, the old war slogans change. It's now "When Johnny Comes Nodding Home," and there is an ironic symbolism in the fact that fund raising for disabled veterans is often through the sale of poppies.

9 Junking Junk

Well, what's to be done? Certainly conditions are getting worse. The number of addicts, and the amount of addict-related crime, prostitution, VD, and police prosecution and political corruption are increasing. Obviously, there are no short-term solutions, only a few stop-gap measures. Let me mention a few stop-gap measures—not solutions:

In the context that current U.S. addiction programs of any nature, no matter how expanded, are not likely to "improve" more than 30 percent of all addicts, I would support to *a degree* what has been called by New York Assemblyman Antonio Olivieri a "heroin transition program" which would be aimed at taking the addict out of the realm of crime and moving him/her into the area of medical treatment. In effect the program would offer heroin by prescription to induce addicts to come into treatment into specially controlled and licensed clinics. Heroin distribution would be carefully monitored to prevent illegal heroin diversion. To insure that only "bona fide" addicts were receiving the prescribed heroin, footprints of the addict would be taken to insure accurate identification. Footprints, rather than fingerprints, would be used, to avoid any connection with law-enforcement agencies, which might try to avail themselves of the clinic's files.

Obviously, for such a program to get off the ground, federal, state, and local regulations would have to be re-written in order to prescribe heroin legally, even under carefully controlled settings. This would leave all other heroin transactions illegal. Hopefully, other law-enforcement agencies would work to cut down illegal supplies. With some of the profit removed from heroin by its semi-legalization, perhaps more law-enforcement officials could then concentrate on catching upper-echelon pushers rather than profiting from them.

Once the addict is in a heroin transition program, he/she may be motivated to shift to methadone—as happens often in British clinics.

Again, like heroin, methadone dispensing would have to be carefully monitored, including footprint identification to prevent illegal diversion.

Once the addict doesn't have to spend his entire day scrounging and stealing for a fix, he/she may be able to get some job training and counseling. As Olivieri says, "a halfway house for those who have never been willing to come halfway before." As methadone authority Nat Hentoff says: "And those who take that step, it is expected, will no longer have to stalk the rest of the citizenry to get their fix."

A substantial and legitimate source of opposition to even the tightly controlled legalization of heroin is black, Puerto Rican, and Chicano community leaders who believe, in large part correctly, that such a program is an especially malevolent form of white racism aimed at tranquilizing and subduing their people. These community leaders believe that such programs, instead of getting at fundamental socioeconomic injustices which are patently obvious, will turn hundreds of thousands of young addicts into "legal zombies."

If heroin maintenance or transition programs do not provide for meaningful social reform for the addict in terms of income supplements, health care, housing, nutrition, and education, one must agree that legalized heroin will "waste" hundreds of thousands of addicts. On the plus side of the argument for controlled legalization is the fact that the present addict situation is getting worse. Thousands of addicts die every year and those that do not die are sick, debilitated, and criminalized. The rising profits of illegal heroin *insure* that the situation can only worsen and *increase* the number of addicts. In New York City alone last year 1259 people died of narcotic-related causes. Continued illegalization can only increase the number of addicts. Continued illegalization can only increase the number of those deaths. Partial legalization, at least, will end virtually all the deaths.

Those who fear that the controlled, legal dispensing of heroin *might* result in more heroin addicts, must be countered with the fact that continued illegalization will *guarantee* an increase in the number of heroin addicts and heroin addict deaths and diseases.

Of historical relevance to the point of legalization of narcotics is the Japanese experience in Formosa. *The Washington Monthly* of June 1971 reports that "When the Japanese took control of Formosa in 1895, they found a huge addiction problem. The illegal opium trade boomed throughout the Far East, thanks to police complicity, and there were more than 200,000 addicts on Formosa. The Japanese instituted a government opium monopoly. Licensed smokers were permitted to buy their supplies from government shops at fixed low prices adapted to the income level of the consumer. The opium dispensed in these shops was of good quality and carefully prepared. Licensed users were provided with purchase books in which records of amounts dispensed were kept. By 1938 the addict population of 200,000 in 1895 had dropped to 20,000, with very few under the age of 40 years old. Legalization of the narcotic had removed its profitability and thus the impetus for its expansion, consequently the addict population decreased. Unfortunately, by 1939, when the Chinese Nationalists (Kuomintang, KMT), having been thrown out of mainland China, came to Formosa and seized control of the government, they returned to the narcotic prohibition system. Addiction went underground, narcotic profits rose, as did the number of addicts."

While heroin addiction is considered by many so-called legal and social authorities to be a victimless crime, there can be no doubt that heroin's illegalization has created an army of both criminals and victims.

However, any new heroin-transition or heroin-maintenance program must bear the burden of proof that it will not produce zombies, that it will not make the addicts prisoners of their habits or of the state.

Other areas of opposition to such a legalized heroin program will come from those who have a financial and emotional stake in "total-cure" or "drug-free" programs. While being drug free is certainly a worthwhile goal, it is all too obvious that such programs have no meaning for 70 to 90 percent of all addicts, which in effect writes off the vast majority of addicts.

Others oppose any form of legalized heroin program because it would imply a government sanction or approval for heroin. But then rat poison is legal and hardly sanctioned.

Another area of opposition to heroin transition or maintenance, as pointed out by Commissioner Graham Finney of New York's Addiction Services Agency, comes from the "pharmaceutical industry's insistence on promoting profit making drug taking (rather than legal and profitless heroin) to solve virtually all personal problems."

Still another area of resistance to heroin-maintenance programs is found in the addicted for whom, under the scarifying conditions of a racist, sexist, oppressive society, "scoring" is a challenging occupation. Such a life can almost give meaning to the existence of some addicts. Even granting such people the gloomiest of prognoses, it seems highly unlikely that they will opt for the lives they can barely lead now, if they could get heroin legally.

The idea of heroin-transition clinics has recently gained recognition from some unlikely sources. At least on an experimental basis, they have been supported by U.S. Attorney Whitney N. Seymour, Jr., and New York City's Police Commissioner Murphy, who have respectively said:

"I'm positively in favor of an experiment (with a heroin-transition program)" and "I see nothing wrong with a carefully controlled, medically supervised demonstration experiment." (Both quotes in *The New York Times*, February 27, 1972.

Also endorsing such an experiment is District Attorney Frank Hogan and Joseph Califano, former presidential advisor to Lyndon Johnson. While one can hardly be enthusiastic about a heroin maintenance program simply because of endorsements from people like Hogan, Califano, Seymour and Murphy, the program should not be rejected simply on the basis of guilt by association.

Nor for that matter should the program be supported simply because of some of its more reactionary and racist opponents. For example, heroin-maintenance clinics are hardly a new American phenomenon. Between 1912 and 1925 narcotic-maintenance clinics were dispensing low-cost morphine and heroin to addicts in over forty American cities. There was no doubt that many of these clinics cut significantly into the illegal narcotics market, and put large numbers of addicts into contact with physicians. Those addicts availing themselves of the clinic committed no crimes and suffered no morbidity such as hepatitis, malnutrition, or tetanus. At any rate the American Medical Association (AMA) in 1924 urged federal and state governments "to exert their full powers and authority to put an end to all manner of so-called out-patient methods of treatment of addiction." As a result of AMA pressure the clinics were closed.

The AMA's action against heroin maintenance clinics stands out in strong contrast to their failure to oppose "alcohol maintenance clinics," commonly known as saloons and bars, in spite of the fact that legal alcohol kills far more than illegal heroin. This should not be surprising in view of the AMA's current multi-million dollar investments in two major breweries.

Kenneth Brodney, in his 1972 testimony before the New York State Assembly's Ad Hoc Committee on Victimless [*sic*] Crimes on the subject of heroin, stated:

"First, the effect, if not the intent of the antiheroin laws, and their social function today is as an Establishment political weapon to harass, punish and control, particularly the young and the black and the Spanish-speaking poor. (Just look at New York City's over-crowded jails: 90 to 95 percent black and Puerto Rican; 55 to 70 percent addicts.) And this is so because the laws are unfair, and I think unconstitutional (violating the 14th Amendment guarantee of equal protection of the law), since the use of heroin as a psychic pain-killer—primarily by these poor —is totally prohibited and harshly punished, while the psychic pain-killers of the middle and upper classes, such as tranquilizers and barbiturates, are legally available with a doctor's prescription."

As Dr. Henry Lennard of the Langley-Porter Institute points out, "We must stress the *mutuality* of our dilemma with drugs, not the differences between groups who look to drugs for on-the-spot relief from existential pain within a society that emphasizes things at the expense of feelings."

"Second," Mr. Brodney continued, "the laws against heroin possession of even small amounts for personal use turn the user automatically into a criminal. He/she is then led deeper into more serious crime by the cost of feeding a habit made enormously expensive only by its illegality. Both these mechanisms that actually create criminals are the height of irrationality, are totally unnecessary, and run completely counter to the interests of everyone, including both the addict victims and the victims of addict crime."

The particulars of the current experiment that Seymour and Murphy are tentatively supporting were designed by the Vera Institute and the Ford Foundation's Drug Abuse Council and are similar to Olivieri's. The experiment contains the following proposals:

1. Heroin would be used as a "lure" for a few hundred male addicts aged twenty-one to twenty-five with at least a two-year history of heroin addiction. All participants would have either failed in a methadone program or never applied for treatment anywhere.

2. After receiving daily heroin injections for at least three months but not more than six, participants would be moved to methadone, into a drug-free "therapeutic" community, or to a narcotic antagonist such as cyclazocine.

3. Heroin would be dispensed only in the clinic. The program would have psychiatric, educational, and vocational services.

As briefly described, such an experimental program, while headed in the right direction in terms of de-criminalizing heroin, has numerous areas of inadequacies which must be corrected before it could gain even a semblance of community support. As the program stands now it isn't much better than what Congressman Charles B. Rangel of Harlem called it, "a colonialist type of thinking in dealing with the natives' problems, i.e., it does nothing to cure the natives' illness, it just protects the status quo from being endangered from that illness. But if the fascination with colonial type heroin maintenance persists, then why don't we set up heroin clinics in the military, rather than the ghetto. Certainly the Army presents the ideal controlled environment for just such an experiment." Stewart Alsop in *Newsweek* said that, "Such a program aimed at the ghetto would put the government into the business of poisoning people, mostly poor, young and black people."

That the Drug Abuse Council should have some inadequacies shouldn't exactly be surprising, given the makeup of its founder and board members:

1. McGeorge Bundy—former presidential advisor and developer of the U.S. counterinsurgency efforts in Vietnam.

2. William R. Hewlett—president of Hewlett-Packard—a prominent Department of Defence contractor for the "electronic battlefield" throughout Indochina.

3. Eddie N. Williams—vice-president for public affairs, University of Chicago—infamous for its slum-land-lordism.

4. J. Henry Smith—president of the Equitable Life Assurance Society, which played a key role with other members of the medical-industrial complex in significantly contributing to the inflationary spiral of health costs, thus depriving people of health care. Not surprisingly, such people as those listed above, as well as Commissioner

Murphy and U.S. Attorney Seymour, support such a program more as an attempt to prevent crime against white citizens, than to rehabilitate ghetto communities and addicts.

Specific criticisms of the above experiment would include:

1. Its obvious sexism in limiting the program to males.

2. Its obvious age chauvinism in limiting the program to those over twenty-one, when a substantial number of addicts are below eighteen years old.

3. Its failure to provide adequate security precautions to prevent illegal diversion of heroin, as happens with methadone clinics.

4. Its failure to include adequate income and housing supplements.

5. Most importantly, the experiment does not deal with any long term sociopolitical issues which created the addiction problem in the first place.

There are a few programs around the country which do emphasize, rather than group therapy or methadone or heroin, political education (PE).

These programs are indigenous to the community and under community-worker control. One such program is the Lincoln Detox Program. While the program's medical function is acute detoxification (withdrawal) from heroin, rather than heroin transition it does provide a model for changing an entire community politically, rather than simply "maintaining," "de-criminalizing," and "sanitizing" addicts.

The program is located in the South Bronx and was formed by a number of local revolutionary organizations, specifically the Black Panther Party, the Young Lords, and the Health Revolutionary Unity Movement. It was their sense that to do any political organizing in the drug-in-

fested South Bronx, they had to confront drugs, and to
confront drugs meaningfully on a community-wide basis
the confrontation and program must be political. Heroin
controls significant portions of virtually everyone's life in
the South Bronx.

Because heroin law-enforcement agencies have institutionalized both the criminal traffic in the drug and the use
of it as but one response to the insanity of America, revolutionary groups, rather than making a psychological analysis of the addict, developed an institutional and political
analysis of the addict and his/her community. The political
analysis states that addiction occurs not because of a certain "personality type" or a "conflicted oedipal complex"
or "ungratified dependency needs" but rather, according to
one of the workers in the program:

"Addiction is a market response to economic dislocation
and class antagonisms. Under capitalism, large corporations, legal and illegal, struggle to evolve and through control of product and marketing techniques, determine
through what channels need shall be directed to feed. In
a corporately controlled society the consumer is corporately directed. Thus needs can be channelled into markets
which can relate satisfaction to specific products.

"Addicts can be seen as a potentially revolutionary
group. Addicts are a lumpen *class*—they don't produce anything but crime . . . Addicts have a keen sense of hardship
and they must stay away from the police." Political organizing efforts then take the form of bringing political
consciousness to the addicts' keen sense of hardship and
explain why both the addicts and the organizers "are fighting the cops."

Dr. Thomas S. Szasz of Upstate Medical Center in Syra-
cuse sees addicts as a specifically scapegoated class or sec-
tor of the population, where scapegoating mechanisms

work quite similarly to racism and sexism. That is, the scapegoats are seen as "nigger addicts." They are seen as a class that:

1. is politically unorganized and hence unable to defend itself.

2. exhibits characteristics generally regarded as defects or diseases or to whom such defects or diseases must be easily attributable. For example, Dr. Jerome H. Jaffe is appointed by President Nixon to head the federal "drug abuse" program. Jaffe is a physician and a psychiatrist. Are we to assume, then, that "drug abuse" is a medical, and in particular, a psychiatric problem and that drug addiction is a disease? Or is it a political-economic problem? According to *The New York Times* Dr. Jaffe is considered an expert on drug addiction because, "When he arrived in Illinois in 1966 from the Bronx there wasn't a single state-supported bed for the treatment of drug addicts in Illinois. The first year he got 300 beds. Now there are 1800." The impetus to make addicts into medical scapegoats has allowed bed-pushers to pose as drug experts, when in fact the overwhelming majority of addicts do not need hospital beds, nor are they helped by being labeled "sick."

But not surprisingly, and indeed consistent with the above, at a recent American Medical Association (AMA) meeting President Nixon assured the AMA that in the fight against drug abuse "America's doctors are indispensable front line soldiers in this all-important battle."

While the medical profession could have at least developed a first-aid manual for dealing with drug-abuse casualties on a short-term basis, they have done no such thing. Nor have any significant number of medical emergency rooms been even willing to attempt to treat persons suffering from heroin overdose or withdrawal or even to develop a "heroin hotline" to provide information for

heroin and overdose emergencies. The failure to develop
such programs contributes significantly to the death rate
of addicts. The kind of information a hotline could provide
would include the fact that if there is one other person
present to give artificial respiration to the overdosed addict, the chances of survival are good. Most medical clinics
and physicians still refuse to provide standard prescription
medications to allow an addict to withdraw without suffering severe physical discomfort and occasionally death.
The fact that the addict has no available medical means
for a medically safe and physically nondisruptive method
of heroin withdrawal keeps addicts hooked longer than
need be.

Moreover, as Dr. Henry L. Lennard in his book, *Mystification and Drug Misuse* points out: "Far from preventing
the spread of drug abuse, the nation's doctors occupy a
key role in a roundelay of mystification about drug misuse
that has made narcotics a minor problem compared to
licit drugs, such as stimulants, tranquilizers, and anti-de-
pressants. *Doctors promote the spread of drug-taking in
society* [emphasis added]. In 1969, as Dr. Lennard points
out, there were 202 million prescriptions for psychoactive
drugs prescribed to a population of about 200 million,
(where each prescription was for an average of at least 40
pills), and these figures do not include prescriptions writ-
ten in hospitals and clinics."

In fact, Dr. Lennard implies a collusion between the
pharmaceutical industry and the medical profession: "The
facts of the matter are that huge profits—surely dwarfing
those of the heroin trade—are being made by an industry
and to a lesser extent an entire profession, to whom we are
supposed to entrust our health and welfare. A quick look
through the great number of medical publications, all of
which are dependent on the pharmaceutical industry's ad-

vertising dollar, will reveal the active part that the drug industry plays in mystifying doctors, not to mention everyone else, about drugs."

Not surprisingly, when one reviews the pharmaceutical industry's early history at the turn of this century, one finds such "ethical" drug firms as The Bayer Company promoting not only aspirin, but also heroin as a "cough-suppressant that does not have the harmful effects of other opiates." The Bayer Company actually used the word "heroin" as a trade name and featured it in national magazine advertisements: "Heroin, the sedative for coughs. Send for samples!"

The current analogy to Bayer aspirin is seen with such drugs as amphetamines. Despite all their differences, amphetamine users, whether on the street or in the kitchen, share one important thing in common—the initial source of supply—the American pharmaceutical industry conduiting the drug through the local physician. James Graham in "Amphetamine Politics on Capitol Hill" (*Transaction,* January 1972) notes that "the drug industry has skillfully managed to convert a chemical with meager medical justification and considerable potential for medical harm, into multi-hundred-million dollar profits. High profits, reaped from such vulnerable and harmful products, require extensive, sustained political efforts for their continued existence. The lawmakers who have declared that possession of marijuana is a serious crime have simultaneously defended and protected the products of the amphetamine pillmakers." In effect the Nixon-supported and passed Comprehensive Drug Abuse Prevention and Control Act of 1970 is a statement of national policy which declares an all-out war on drugs which are *not* a source of *corporate* income. Meanwhile, under the protection of the alleged Control Act billions of amphetamines are overproduced without medical justification, producing symptoms and millions in profits.

At the congressional hearings for the Drug Control Act of 1970, unabashedly the American Medical Association testified that "Amphetamines were among those drugs used daily in practically every physician's armamentarium."

At the same hearing Donald Fletcher, coincidentally former Texas State police officer, but now in charge of distribution protection for Smith, Kline and French laboratories, one of the leading manufacturers of amphetamines, called for "licensing the exporter" but for *no* controls over the shipments themselves.

All this occurred in the face of testimony from Dr. John D. Griffith of Vanderbilt Medical School who said "amphetamines are more widespread, more incapacitating, more dangerous and socially disrupting than heroin addiction—and eight percent of *all* prescriptions are for amphetamines."

The congressional hearings had provided, according to James M. Graham, "considerable testimony to the effect that massive amphetamine production coupled with their illegal diversion posed a major threat to the public's health. No Congressman would argue that this was not the case." However, Congressman Jerome R. Waldie said that while "the House was always ready to combat crime in the streets, it wasn't ready to combat crime that involves a corporation and its profits." Waldie concluded that the Nixon Administration's decision "to favor the profits of the industry over the health of the people is a cruel decision— the consequences of which will be suffered by thousands of young people." As Congressman Robert Giamimo said, "Why should we allow the legitimate [*sic*] drug manufacturer to supply organized crime and pushers by producing more amphetamines than what is medically necessary?"

The answer was supplied by Senator Thomas Eagleton: "When the chips are down, the power of the drug companies is simply more compelling than appeal from the public."

Senator Thomas Dodd declared that federal laws have failed to control the diversion of *lawfully* manufactured drugs. Dodd also recognized the ways in which all Americans had become increasingly involved in drug use and that the people's fascination with pills was by no means an "accidental development." Dodd said that "Multihundred million dollar advertising budgets, frequently the most costly ingredient in the price of a pill, have, pill by pill, led, coaxed and seduced post-World War II generations into the 'freaked-out' drug culture . . . Detail men employed by drug companies propagandize doctors (whose often sole source of drug education is from drug company detail men) into pushing their special brand of palliative. Free drug samples in the doctor's office are as common as inflated fees."

John Wykert of *Medical News* asks, "How well has the medical model or disease model worked in the treatment of the addict?" According to Dr. Donald B. Louria in *Overcoming Drugs*, "The success rate is non-existent."

Sociologist Nicholas Regush, discussing addiction in the context of a medical model and thus as a "sickness," notes that "The addict before 1914, before the Harrison Tax Act, was seen as neither sick nor criminal." Since the passage of the Harrison Tax Act, effectively outlawing heroin, the addict "has been looked upon as a criminal and now in the Age of Benevolence, the addict is viewed as 'sick.' "

To compound matters, physician and psychiatrist Dr. Karl Menninger gives us the remarkable equation that "all criminals are ill," thereby sensitizing us to view anyone

incarcerated for any reason whatsoever as ill. Regush says:
"Clearly the aim of the physician and/or psychiatrist working for government or private agencies is to control the
reality of the addict, to pretend nothing is wrong with
your country, to note that addiction is both a criminal and
a medical-psychological matter and that those who use
drugs should be 'rehabilitated' and re-introduced into
'normal' society."

The Lincoln Detox Program, in an attempt to "de-medi-
calize," de-mystify, de-professionalize and de-monopolize
their antidrug services, have 90 percent of the staff come
from the ranks of ex-addicts, many of whom came through
the Detox program themselves. According to the Health
Policy Advisory Center, "the Detox Program does not want
to be seen as simply the place that dispenses methadone
for detoxification. For that reason, as well as others, it has
instituted political education. The Detox Program does not
dispute the value of providing support for detoxified addicts. Support, however, comes in terms of survival needs
for life in the South Bronx, rather than in terms of estab-
lishing an alternate and distinct 'supportive environment'
or 'therapeutic community.' The Program gets many eligi-
ble addicts onto the welfare rolls, helps locate housing,
and arranges for medical treatment within the hospital. It
also works closely with an organization of ex-addicts who
attempt to organize other addicts around the economic
and political causes of their addiction." The Program is a
social and political advocate for the addict and his/her
community.

The political education (PE) in the Detox program is
offered to both addicts *and* workers in an attempt to break
down artificial "staff-client" barriers and hierarchies. PE
sessions focus on "conditions in the community . . . we are
out to deal with the contradictions and problems of that

class of people." The Detox staff view addiction as a symptom, secondary to socioeconomic causes, rather than as individual neuroses. Thus political education is emphasized and not psychotherapy. While psychotherapy at its benevolent best can be supportive, it nevertheless tends to define the problem of addiction as being a problem for a collection of sick individuals, rather than being a collective problem forced on and faced by an entire class of people.

As Dr. Tom Levin, psychiatrist working in the South Bronx, says, the failure of conventional antiheroin programs "reflects the social and ethical bankruptcy of the professionals in their refusal to accept the validity of ideological and community approaches. The Black Panthers, using politically based antidrug approaches, are effective precisely because of their deep ideological roots and because they have organized their community constituencies. Their basic tenets are a recognition of drug abuse as a form of sociopolitical pathology and the right of any community to organize for its own *social defense.*"

Across the country a number of such "community social defense programs (sometimes called Operation Clean Turf) are arising. They develop from a strong, shared community realization of the social, political, and human costs of heroin addiction. These community groups say, in essence, 'You may use drugs some place else, but you absolutely cannot bring in or push heroin in this community.' They engage in citizens' arrests to supplement and prod ineffective law-enforcement agencies, and they demand of the drug user that he/she receive some form of therapeutic help if he/she is to remain a community member. Their effectiveness is built on community and political organization."

If the heroin-transition experimental program would meet the five objections listed previously, it might secure a greater constituency and eventually expand into a community-wide, community-controlled, politicized version of the British heroin program.

Well, what is the British system for heroin control? According to Dr. Henry Brill, director of Pilgrim State Hospital, the British program in brief is a heroin maintenance and/or transition program somewhat similar to the Drug Abuse Council's experimental program mentioned earlier:

1. Heroin is dispensed at no charge in specially centralized and licensed clinics to registered addicts.

2. Sterile disposable syringes are provided to prevent any infection (hepatitis, tetanus, and malaria).

3. Attempts at a transition program from injectable heroin to oral methadone was a complete failure, i.e., the Dole-Nyswander methadone maintenance program, but substantial transition to injectable methadone was often successful. However, in the majority of cases, heroin remained the drug of choice.

4. Perhaps most importantly, though, heroin is now legally dispensed, *"addiction is no longer on the rise,* and there appears to have been a *decrease* in the last year."
There are now not more than 4000 heroin addicts in Britain, with a population of 50 million, compared to our growing addict population of 600,000 out of a general population of 200 million. Therefore the United States, with its illegal heroin, has 300 addicts per 100,000 general population compared to Britain's 8 addicts per 100,000 general population. On a per capita basis we have over thirty-five times the number of addicts as does Britain.

As William S. Burroughs, author of *The Naked Lunch,* and a former heroin addict for fifteen years, says: "Thanks to our efficient Federal Narcotics Bureau, police action against addicts has been carried further than in any other country of the world, and yet we've got more per capita use of heroin than any nation of the world. This would seem to a rational observer to at least suggest the hypothesis that police repression and increased penalties are not the answers and in fact are part of the problem."

Burroughs tells how he stopped his addiction:

"While I was in England and could obtain all the heroin I wanted by prescription, I was able to gain control of my own life. While I was in the U.S. under the fatherly protection of the Narcotics Bureau, I found it quite impossible to kick my habit. And I tried eleven times."

5. There is virtually no crime in Britain associated with heroin addiction.

6. Also there is virtually no disease or death, prostitution or VD, police, prosecution or political corruption associated with heroin in the British system.

On the critical side of the program is the fact that only 25 percent of the addicts were doing a full week's work. However, in a few clinics where job training was available, 40 to 60 percent of the addicts were working at least on a half-time basis. Of course in the United States virtually no addict does a half week's work, let alone a full week's work. In Britain, significant and adequate housing, income maintenance, and occupational training are not available. And worst of all, no political education is available. As Dr. Tom Levin points out in *Social Policy*, without correct political education and action a heroin maintenance program is "basically a way of cutting consciousness, breeding apathy and destroying social involvement and action." With the government becoming the "pusher" and "sole supplier," the government is in a uniquely powerful position to control, or at least manipulate, large segments of the population.

By having the heroin and/or methadone dispensed by a community-controlled, politically conscious program, government control and/or manipulation may be considerably lessened. For example, the community, more than the government, would have a much greater stake in preventing illegal diversions of heroin and/or methadone.

Dr. LeClair Bissell of New York's Roosevelt Hospital has also reviewed the British system and makes the following points:

1. The program does not so much treat addicts as it does control the supply of heroin. While certainly an improvement over our system, it is, again, only a stop-gap measure, not a solution. However, by centralizing and limiting the number of heroin-dispensing clinics, the supply of heroin has clearly been controlled.

2. Unfortunately, since the heroin is so tightly controlled, with stringent requirements for admission to the heroin-maintenance program, some addicts aren't admitted to the program and must turn to crime to purchase expensive black-market heroin. Clearly a program that wishes to eliminate criminality and profit from heroin must dispense the heroin to those who crave it, to prevent a profitable black market.

The heroin bargaining game begins when an "addict comes to a clinic and his doctor is unable to tell by simply examining the patient and taking his history how much heroin he needs." If at the beginning of the doctor-patient relationship, the physician does not trust the addict, the addict will attempt to bargain for so many grains of heroin and the doctor will offer so many grains less until a "satisfactory" compromise is reached. On the other hand, if the doctor overestimates the amount of drug needed by the addict, the excess is then available to give to friends or to sell in the black market. If the doctor underestimates, the addict must continue to obtain part of his supply illegally. If the initial amount given is correct, the doctor will often neglect to recognize that increasing tolerance may develop and the addict may require increasing amounts of drug.

How then should these problems be dealt with?

First of all the addict should be initially and then periodically admitted to the hospital in order to assess carefully the appropriate dosage under very strictly controlled conditions.

Secondly, all heroin should be "shot-up" under the strict supervision of a health worker to insure that the heroin is not being diverted to illegal markets, even if this means the addict must return three or four times every day for a period of years. The development of long acting synthetic heroin may eliminate the need to shoot up more than once a day or once a week.

In effect, of course, if heroin is legally available through a physician, then all euphoric drugs must be, to avoid reproducing the illegalization-profit-criminal cycle. In addition the drug must be available essentially free of charge, or else the poor, ghetto addict will be forced to continue his/her criminal life in order to purchase the drug. The drug itself must be under community control to prevent outside, hostile political forces from using the drug for control of the community.

Thirdly, adequate income, housing, and social services would eliminate some of the need for the addict to become involved in diverting heroin for black-market profiteering.

Fourth, the clinic and its services must be available on a twenty-four-hour-per-day, seven-days-a-week basis.

3. Fortunately in Britain, because the quality of heroin dispensed is high, as well as free, addicts clearly prefer to avoid the black market. By the same token, given the high quality of legal heroin, the addict is less likely to make the transition to methadone or a heroin antagonist such as cyclazocine.

4. By having a few clinics highly dispersed throughout a city, the addicts themselves would be more dispersed instead of congregating together, as they do now in certain neighborhoods where they know illegal drugs are more easily obtained. Drug addicts are not necessarily or naturally drawn to each other. They often meet just to find drugs.

In Britain the addict qualifies as a patient under the National Health Service in order to receive his/her heroin. Thus he/she has not only no need to become a thief and/or a prostitute, but no need to become part of the underworld-addict subculture. There is no need for the addict to maximize his/her anonymity and mobility.

5. As Nat Hentoff points out: "By learning more about how each addict-patient reacts to various therapies and programs while on heroin, we may be able to find out a great deal more about realistic methods of treatment. Some addicts function very well on heroin; some function badly. I've known addicts who have managed to keep their habits fairly small and who have worked efficiently for years." There might be more of that kind of "nondisabled" addict if the getting of drugs wasn't so associated with the possibility of panic. Many addicts now are affected by fear of not being able to get enough heroin next time. So they shoot up whatever they can get when they can get it. Dr. Robert Gould, director of Adolescent Services at Bellevue Psychiatric Hospital, says that "many addicts want to escalate their dose for psychological reasons, but the notion of an absolute physical need to increase the dose is a myth. I know people who are well stabilized on heroin, including successful lawyers and Wall Street stockbrokers." Dr. Burt D'Lugoff of Johns Hopkins School of Medicine explained that stabilization of heroin dosages was and is attained simply by using an adequate and appropriate dose of a

steady quantity of heroin at regular intervals "which, after a few weeks, produced only mild euphoria and very little nodding or withdrawal pains, and more importantly, permitted the addict to function essentially normally as many heroin addicts have demonstrated."

New York Assemblyman Andrew Stein has pointed out that one of the major causes of rising welfare rolls are "the large number of addicts in the disabled category." Conceivably, at least, if heroin maintenance were available for these "disabled" people they would no longer be disabled. If meaningful work with an adequate income was available for them they would no longer be on the welfare rolls.

On the other hand, when Jule Sugarman, the head of New York City's welfare programs, proclaims that addicts are "paralyzing" the city's welfare program, he's failing to make the connection that the inadequate welfare system is in fact one of the contributing factors to the rising addiction rate and that they are inter-related, in a vicious cycle. The New York State budget for 1971–1972, in spite of an $800 million increase, nevertheless *cut back* welfare allotments by 10 percent.

And still further along, it will take far more money than simply the expenses of welfare allotments to develop a heroin-methadone-transition-maintenance program *with* serious and relevant social services. Such services have to be extensive and expensive enough to include not only service for the addict, but indeed rehabilitation of the addicts' community, i.e., taking serious steps to wipe out poverty, poor housing, no medical care, etc. When one begins to talk about services that are so broad ranging, then the heroin-methadone-maintenance aspects fall into insignificance and the programs for social change, aiming at the *causes* of the addiction, become the significant services.

Of course if the services are truly supportive, they will be extremely attractive, encouraging people to become addicts to get the services. Therefore the services must be available on a community-wide basis, so that one doesn't have to become an addict in order to get housing, food, and medical maintenance.

By the same token, the failure to develop such community-wide, community-controlled services in the first place has undoubtedly contributed to the ghetto residents' susceptibility to the heroin influx. The kinds of serious political changes that would be required to eliminate widespread poverty are obviously not going to come about without a protracted and intensive political struggle of a nonlegislative variety.

Because the British heroin clinics are dispensing centers rather than treatment or rehabilitative centers, there is little incentive to experience any discomfort, let alone begin a work program and become politically active. The clinics simply place no demands on the addict, but rather the other way around, to the point where the addict can "opt for an inpatient unit where he can remain for many months, be very comfortable and have all his immediate needs met."

As one addict reported, "It's better to be a junkie than a nothing." One shouldn't oppose this situation on the basis of a puritanical work ethic, but on the political grounds that such a program can only serve the status quo and is in effect literally a pharmaceutical pacification program.

Ultimately, of course, political problems can't be solved with pills, legal or otherwise, but only by political action. Pills may serve the pill industry, they don't serve the people. Any traditional, current, conventional notions of rehabilitation are, as sociologist Nicholas Regush says, "simply an outmoded and absurd response to the propen-

sity of the Corporate-Welfare state to single out those
individuals who do not contribute to the state's search for
mindless efficiency and either to incarcerate them or to
confine them to 'rehabilitation' centers."

As John Wicklein of New York's station WRVR says
"The only long term care of heroin addiction is a radical
change in the American way of life; an end to the unequal
distribution of wealth and to the racism and sexism that
has brought that about. Good will will not change anything. Only concerted political action will."

Up until 1949 the Chinese people were effectively addicted and exploited by colonizers. As the Committee of
Concerned Asian Scholars points out: "After 1949, when
the Chinese once and for all threw out the foreigners they
also developed effective methods to eliminate the ravages
of opium-heroin. China is not only the land to suffer most
deeply at the hands of the drug. It is also the society which
has effectively eliminated it as a problem. Elimination of
the drug traffic and addiction was brought about totally,
rapidly and humanely in the People's Republic of China.
Contrary to conventional wisdom in the U.S., the Chinese
recognized that the social political system, not individual
sickness or aberration, lay at the root of the problem.
Therefore, drastic political and social changes, as well as
changes in the attitudes and life situations of individuals,
were essential. The new government which values people
above profits entirely eliminated the involvement of the
Western powers and their indigenous helpers. Swift and
uncompromising crackdowns destroyed the entire corrupt
network of traders and pushers.

"More significantly, the Chinese provided new opportunities for addicts to rehabilitate themselves. Addicts were
not seen as personally guilty or deranged. They were not
viewed as criminals but rather as victims of the corrupt
old system. What counted was helping them understand

that they were victims of the old order and that extraordinary opportunities awaited them and all oppressed people in a new society which they would help to shape. Free drugs were provided for registered addicts in programs of rapidly phased withdrawal. This was accompanied by intensive political education and discussion about their personal problems and how they derived from the old society and what they must change for the new. The victims of addiction then received job education and opportunities. They were not treated to sermons about their personal failures and then sent back to the filth, degradation and despair of ghetto life where addiction provided the only relief. Moral rearmament, Christian, therapeutic, or any other kind which leaves untouched the political roots of oppression is a cruel mockery of a cure as millions of U.S. addicts have learned. Nor were Chinese addicts permanently fixed on some miracle drug offering the prospect of lifetime addiction as many methadone advocates now suggest. Meaningful, non-exploitative work and communal relations among equals were open to men and women who were prepared to break with the old order. By the mid-1950s China's millions of addicts had been successfully reintegrated into a dynamic, developing, and hopeful society.

"China was able to solve its addiction problem by starting to build, from the bottom up, a new society. A revolution for life in America will hardly be the same as China's. But no matter how long it takes and hard it seems, fighting for a better life is the only hope there is."

If nothing else we must always be cognizant of the fact that as long as oppression and poverty, racism and sexism remain integral parts of our society, heroin (or something stronger) will always be in demand. Making it legal or illegal only changes its price and source of distribution, not its availability.

Heroin addiction is not a criminal problem, though

criminals and crime are involved. Nor is heroin addiction a medical problem, though medical symptoms are produced. Heroin addiction is ultimately a political and economic problem created by, and controlled for, wealthy criminals with political connections, political officials with corporate and criminal connections, and corporate officials controlling the priorities of our society. If corporate America remains unchanged, the demand for heroin (or other euphorics) will increase in spite of attempts at its selective suppression and because of attempts to use heroin to suppress selectively, both politically and personally. Heroin manufacturing, distribution, and usage occur in a well-defined political context. Until that political context is destroyed, heroin and its concomitant diseases and deaths, crime and corruption, will remain part of our daily lives.

Acknowledgments

Acknowledgment is made to the following to reprint by permission excerpted material under their control and/or for their publishing material containing information critical to sections of this book.

The New York Times, copyright by The New York Times Co.
  "A Try at Heroin Clinics Wins Increasing Support"
      by JAMES M. MARKHAM, 2/27/72.
  "Police Scandals Spreading: Officials Believe Much Corruption Is Still Uncovered"
      by DAVID BURNHAM, 1/28/72.
  "Study Finds Black Market Developing in Methadone"
      by JAMES M. MARKHAM, 1/2/72.
  "Do You Know Any 12-Year-Old Junkies?"
      by CHARLES B. RANGEL, 1/4/72.
  "Behind Police Corruption"
      by ADAM WALINSKY, 11/12/72.
  "Panel Told How Addicts Stole-to-Order for Police"
      by JAMES M. MARKHAM, 10/28/71.
  "Chemical Warfare Drugs Called Possible Aid to Heroin Addicts"
      by DANA ADAMS SCHMIDT, 11/23/71.
  "Flying Drug-Runners Reap Big Profits"
      by ROBERT LINDSEY, 11/30/71.

The New York Times Magazine, copyright by The New York Times Co.
  "G.I.'s and O.J.'s in Vietnam"
    by NORMAN E. ZINBERG, M.D., 12/5/71.
The Nation, copyright by The Nation Co.
  "The Cops Can't Find the Pusher"
    by K. SCOTT CHRISTIANSON, 11/29/71.
  "The Golden Arm of the Law"
    by WILLIAM P. BROWN, 10/25/71.
  "Uncle Sam, Pusher"
    by DAVID KASHIMBA, 9/20/71.
  "The Catch in Amnesty"
    by SAMUEL A. SIMON, 10/4/71.
The Village Voice, copyright by The Village Voice, Inc.
  "Heroin Hearing: The Price of Illegality"
    by KENNETH BRODNEY, 3/2/72.
  "Dealing With Heroin Now: How to Begin"
    by NAT HENTOFF, 2/17/72.
  "The Land of the Freaks and the Home of the Dung"
    by PAUL HOFFMAN, 9/23/71.
The New England Journal of Medicine, copyright by The Massachusetts Medical Society.
  "Drugs, Doctors and Deceit"
    by THOMAS S. SZASZ, M.D., 1/13/72.
New York Law Journal, copyright by New York Law Publishing Co.
  "State Commission Reports on Police and Courts"
    by PAUL J. CURRAN, 12/6/71.
  "Lawmen's Best Efforts Fail to Curb Narcotics on Street"
    by WHITNEY NORTH SEYMOUR, JR., 12/6/71.
The Progressive, copyright by The Progressive, Inc.
  "The Great Drug Education Hoax"
    by SEYMOUR HALLECK, M.D., 1970 reprint.
Monthly Review, copyright by Monthly Review, Inc.
  "The Political Economy of Junk"
    by SOL YURICK, Dec. 1970.

Newsweek, copyright by Newsweek, Inc.
  "Chicago's Black Vigilantes," 9/27/72.
New York, copyright by NYM Corp.
  "The Case Against District Attorney Hogan"
    by MARTIN GARBUS, 12/6/71.
P.I.C. News, copyright by The Public Information Center.
  "Dealing in Dope"
    by JEFF KAMEN, Jan./Feb. 1971.
Earth Magazine, copyright by Earth Publications, Inc.
  "CIA Dope Calypso"
    by ALLEN GINSBERG, Mar. 1972.
Earth News, copyright by Earth Publications, Inc.
  "CIA Exposed in 'Operation Jones,'" Feb. 8, 1972.
Laos: War and Revolution, copyright by Harper and Row, Inc.
  "Opium and Politics in Laos"
    by DAVID FEINGOLD. Edited by NINA S. ADAMS and ALFRED
    W. MC COY, 1970.
Ramparts, copyright by Noah's Ark, Inc.
  "The New Opium War"
    by FRANK BROWNING and BANNING GARRETT, May 1971.
  "Sports"
    by JACK SCOTT, Nov. 1971.
The National Enquirer, copyright by Best Medium Publishing,
Inc.
  "TV Creates a Drug Culture in U.S."
    by SENATOR GAYLORD NELSON, 1/2/72.
Social Policy, copyright by International Arts and Sciences
Press, Inc.
  "New Myths About Drug Programs"
    by TOM LEVIN, Sept./Oct., 1971.
Civil Liberties, copyright by The American Civil Liberties
Union.
  "Abusing Drug Abusers: The Military Solution"
    by BOB and CAROL SPENCER, Nov. 1971.
The Opium Trail: Heroin and Imperialism, copyright and writ-
ten by Committee of Concerned Asian Scholars, 1971.

Penthouse, copyright by Penthouse International Ltd.
  "How to Silence the Black Minority" (Parts I and II)
    by WILLIAM R. CORSON, Dec. 1970 and Jan. 1971.
Dispatch News Service, copyright by Dispatch News Service.
  "Drug Trade Rocks Asia: Officials Involved"
    by T. D. ALLMAN, 1/29/72.
Liberation News Service, copyright by LNS News Service, Inc.
  "Rent-A-Narc: 'He Was A Joy To Work With,'" 4/8/72.
  "The New Police Technology: Bringing the Boys Home from Vietnam"
    by ROBERT BARKAN, 1/19/72.
  "Politics of the White Drug Plague"
    by MICHAEL ROSSMAN, 8/7/71.
  "How to Win Friends and Influence People: CIA Uses Threat of Starvation in Laos," 9/4/71.
  "Shooting Up Malaria . . . A New Problem," 4/10/71.
  "Southeast Asia's Newest Addicts: U.S. Embassy Kids Hooked on Heroin"
    by THOMAS MARLOWE, 9/29/71.
  "Smack and the Superhero"
    by BENHARI, 10/20/71.
  "White Lightning: An Interview With Revolutionary Ex-Addicts"
    by LIBERATED GUARDIAN staff, 1/8/72.

Index